To Cindy and Andy,

"Going Kosher" what a
wonderful idea!

Any questions please call

Love,
Devrah and Rabbi
Hilsenrath

We are all guests in God's kitchen...

GOING KOSHER IN 30 DAYS
RABBI ZALMAN GOLDSTEIN

FIRST EDITION
Copyright ©2007

The
JEWISH
Learning Group

Tel. 1-(888)-56-LEARN
www.JewishLearningGroup.com
info@JewishLearningGroup.com

ISBN-10: 1-891293-23-0
ISBN-13: 978-1-891293-23-8

Dedicated to my children

Mendel, Manya, Chana'le, Hindy, and Dovid Moshe

NOTE TO READERS

This book is an introduction to the kosher dietary laws and is intended to acquaint readers with the world of kosher living. As comprehensive as it is, it should not be substituted for a full, in-depth study of the subject. Any questions that arise should be presented to a competent kosher expert who can also teach you the customs of your community.

Acknowledgements

Writing this book was a thoroughly daunting yet very enjoyable experience. So much has already been written about kosher; indeed, the wellsprings never end. The challenge has been distilling rivers of information into a concise, logical, step-by-step format, while maintaining a balance between delivering too much information and too little. If this balance is found in the pages of this book, it is due to all the people who contributed by reading, editing, and refining the material.

I owe a special debt of gratitude to Rabbi Sholom Ber Chaikin of Beachwood, Ohio, a noted *Halachic* (Jewish legal) authority who reviewed the entire work to ensure its meticulous compliance with Jewish law.

I am very thankful to my wife Devorah, for her editorial assistance and continuous encouragement, making the entire writing process more pleasant and enjoyable.

To Rabbis Chaim Fogelman and Yitzchak Hanoka, kosher law experts of OK KOSHER CERTIFICATION, one of the largest Kosher Certification agencies in the world, for reviewing the book, allowing us all to benefit from their many combined years of experience.

To Yehudis Cohen, Stephen Delaney, Leibel Estrin, Rabbi Aharon Goldstein, Rabbi Levi Y. Goldstein, Rashi & Leah Handwerger, Moshe & Deborah Haratz, Rabbi Sholtiel Lebovic of GO KOSHER AMERICA, Rabbi Don Yoel Levy of OK KOSHER CERTIFICATION, Mordechai Olesky, Chana Shloush, and Rabbi Eliyahu Touger for reading, editing, commenting, and contributing. To Esther Blau, Tzivia Emmer, Dr. Velvl Greene, Leah Lederman, and Vivian Perez for adding sugar and spice.

To Aryeh Friedman of JF DESIGNS for assistance with the cover design.

To the many people who shared their personal notes and experiences in the "PEOPLE'S QUOTES" sprinkled throughout this book.

And to all the other countless people who are not mentioned by name. You all have my unending gratitude!

Menu

SECOND COURSE — *SHOPPING KOSHER*

Introduction

*E*veryone enjoys reading about food, and studying the laws of keeping kosher shouldn't be any different. If you visit any Jewish bookstore, chances are that you'll find a dizzying number of titles devoted to many aspects of kosher living. You will see information on making your kitchen kosher, shopping kosher, the kosher diet and the Jewish soul, kosher in the *Talmud*, and kosher for Passover, not to mention all kinds of kosher cookbooks!

I'm Jewish, so naturally I'm eager to go kosher, but I haven't the faintest clue where to begin!

LINDA M., AGE 31
BERKELEY, CA

For someone seeking a simple, easy-to-read guide that will explain what it means to keep kosher and show them how to do it, so many book choices can be overwhelming, never mind expensive!

GOING KOSHER IN 30 DAYS was written with the newcomer in mind. It is a down-to-earth introduction that will help you launch your own path to kosher observance at your own pace, and all in one book!

During each of the thirty days, you'll learn another aspect of kosher living. At the end (or is it the beginning?), you will understand how to keep kosher in a way that leads to both physical satisfaction and deeper spiritual fulfillment.

While not an exhaustive study of the "everything-you'll-ever-need-to-know-about-keeping-kosher-for-the-rest-of-your-life" variety, this book will help you get started today. Of course, at some point you should go back to the store to check out the other books on the topic!

IS KEEPING KOSHER DIFFICULT?

Keeping kosher is not difficult at all, yet it does require thought and dedication. With a basic understanding of the kosher dietary laws, and some practice, kosher observance becomes second nature and quite easy to maintain. What's more, thanks to the ever increasing availability of kosher food products, keeping kosher is easier today than ever before in history.

KOSHER 1-2-3

Even though "kosher" as a general topic may sound complex to some, its fundamentals boil down to three basic ideas:

1) The animals, fowl, fish, and other foods that a Jew is permitted or forbidden to eat, and the prescribed method of slaughter and salting for kosher animals and fowl.

2) The separation of meat from dairy foods.

3) The ability for mankind to transform physical food into a vehicle for holiness.

Each of these ideas will be visited in more detail in the following chapters. Within this context, it's interesting to note that almost all Jewish observances are associated with food. From blessings said before and after eating, to the special foods associated with various holidays, keeping kosher permeates one's entire Jewish experience.

STOCKING A KOSHER PANTRY – EASY!

For those who think that being kosher-observant means going hungry most of the time, consider this:

- Over eleven million people will buy kosher food this year, and the numbers are growing. This number includes non-Jews who prefer kosher food as well.

- Your average supermarket carries nearly 25,000 kosher items.

Keeping kosher seemed so complicated and difficult until I saw how easy it really is.

JAY R., AGE 44
MIAMI, FL

- More than 100,000 food products are kosher-certified, including many household brands such as General Mills, Procter & Gamble, Tropicana, Kraft, Post, Heinz, Green Giant, and Hunt's.

- Some 15,000 food manufacturers have obtained kosher certification for their products in the past decade alone, and more are joining every day.

In the 19th century (and earlier), if you wanted to keep kosher, you had to either make the food yourself or simply do without many processed food items. Obviously, this required a lot of commitment, dedication, and courage. Today, however, you can shop at most supermarkets across the country and fill a pantry with name brand, high-quality items that are kosher, tasty, and reasonably priced.

EATING "GOD PARTICLES"

The Torah states, *"Man does not live by bread alone, but by the word of God"* (Deuteronomy 8:3). According to our Sages, when a person consumes food, the body is nourished by the nutrients in the food, while the soul "subsists" on the Godly spark contained within the food. It is not the food itself that bestows "life"; it is this spark of Godliness that sustains the soul and binds it to the body. Thus, a Jew who is careful to eat only kosher foods enlivens his Jewish soul in a powerful way, allowing it to illuminate fully from within, and ultimately positively affecting those around him.

YOU ARE WHAT YOU EAT

Jewish mystical teachings explain that the process of eating is much more than the simple physical act of satiating our hunger. The food we eat ultimately impacts our very essence. Judaism teaches that the food we eat not only affects our bodies;

it influences our soul. Modern science recognizes that food is absorbed into the very flesh and blood of our bodies and that "we become what we eat." The kosher dietary laws direct and guide this connection of body and soul so that both are strong and healthy.

SPIRITUAL REFINEMENT

The *Talmud* teaches that every human activity represents an opportunity for spiritual refinement because, as Jews, we have the Godly-given ability to infuse the physical with holiness and completely transform it in the process. For example, if you donate money that you earned to a worthy cause, the act of charity takes the mundane activity of work and elevates it to a much higher level, spiritualizing everything that went into it. What is true regarding our daily activities is also true of the food we eat.

NON-KOSHER FOOD: SPIRITUAL NOVOCAINE!

Jewish tradition teaches that the forbidden foods referred to in the Torah contain spiritual essences that adversely affect the Jewish soul and numb its spiritual sensitivity. Thus, eating these foods weakens one's faith. For example, by eating birds of prey or other carnivorous animals, one can "absorb" their hostile nature, and as a result, fall under the influence of the creatures' aggressive characteristics.

In contrast, a Jew who eats only kosher meats from permitted animals and fowl will absorb the positive attributes found in the permitted animals, and thereby can become a more purified, refined, and holy person.

Fortunately, you don't have to give up the taste of forbidden food just because you've stopped eating it. The *Talmud* (*Chullin* 109b) teaches that for every non-kosher food, there is an equally savory kosher counterpart!

KOSHER FOREVER

Not long ago, nearly all Jews kept kosher. Only those who wanted to rebel against their religion ate non-kosher food. Today, rampant assimilation and the distractions of the secular world have led Jews who have no intention of rebelling to eat

I find that when I do a mitzvah out of pure faith it is more meaningful for me.

KATHY A., AGE 20
AVENTURA, FL

all kinds of non-kosher food. This happened primarily because they were not taught the beauty and significance of keeping kosher and its vital importance to one's Jewish identity. As Jews, we owe it to ourselves to become educated about our heritage and put what we learn right into practice.

KOSHER & LOGIC

Ultimately, certain Divine *mitzvot* (commandments) in the Torah can never be fully comprehended, including the laws of kosher. In fact, the kosher dietary laws are among the mitzvot called *"chukim"* (statutes), decrees from God that transcend our understanding. Although we can appreciate certain rationales for their observance, we can never plumb the matter to its ultimate depth. While these chukim number fewer than ten out of the entire body of 613 mitzvot, their observance is considered exceedingly important. This is because mitzvot that are observed solely "on faith" (supra-rationally) are the purest demonstration of our faith and dedication to God's Words.

Jews observe the mitzvot of the Torah because they are God's Will, which means that He sets the terms, not we. Yet God does not demand the impossible from us. When we approach mitzvot with an open mind, along with a willingness to explore the truths "beneath the surface," we can come to appreciate their deep beauty and significance to our lives. Additionally, simply being Jewish and having a Jewish soul provides a natural inclination to follow these mitzvot.

LIVING UP TO YOUR FAITH

Ever since the time that God gave the Torah on Mount Sinai, in the year 2448 (1313 BCE), the Jewish people have followed its precepts, even under inconvenient, challenging, or life-threatening circumstances. It is true that true kosher observance requires thought and, at times, extra effort or expense. But keeping kosher is the natural state of existence for a Jew. It is part of a Jew's essence.

Few things in life are more rewarding than being true to oneself and one's faith. Ignoring the soul's call to keep kosher does not really make things easier. It actually sets up a dissonant negative energy that weighs down one's Jewish soul. Compare it to driving a car without oil: you might get where you want to go, but think of the effect on the engine!

MAKING THE DECISION TO GO KOSHER

If you are considering going kosher, the following pages will help you get ready to make the switch. Don't hurry through the book — take one day at a time. In the end, you will be able to make your decision intelligently, and we are confident it will be the right one!

ENCOURAGEMENT

Today, we are fortunate to live in times of unprecedented religious freedom, which makes it infinitely easier to live Jewishly both proudly and openly. Our great-grandparents, by comparison, feared persecution and suffered hardships under despotic regimes; nevertheless, they still practiced Judaism carefully. If while living in an era of religious liberty, we choose not to practice our Judaism fully, what will tomorrow's generation say of us?

Now is as good a time as ever to become a link in the chain of proud, practicing Jews stretching back into history, while reaching far into the future.

May your effort to continue the chain of our great heritage meet with much success, and *ess gezunt* (that's Yiddish for hearty appetite)!

Rabbi Zalman Goldstein
5767/2007

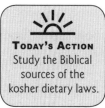

TODAY'S ACTION
Study the Biblical
sources of the
kosher dietary laws.

DAY 1

The History & Origin
of Kosher Law

*T*he kosher dietary laws originate in the Torah ("Five Books of Moses") that was given by God to the Jewish people on Mount Sinai. The Torah, which in Hebrew also means "teaching" and "instruction," is the central and most important document of Judaism. It is considered the "link" between God and the world, containing the historical, ethical, and moral codes we are charged with by God to lead our lives. Living by the values and laws in the Torah allows mankind to rise above the corporeal world and provides the tools to unite the physical and the spiritual. These tools are embodied in the practical *mitzvot* (commandments) of the Torah.

Mitzvot fall into two categories: positive mitzvot tell us what we should do, while prohibitions and "negative" mitzvot tell us what we should refrain from doing. The kosher dietary laws are contained within both of those categories — the foods a Jew is permitted to eat and how they are properly prepared, and the foods and related practices a Jew must avoid.

HISTORICAL PERSPECTIVE

On the 15th of the Hebrew month of Nissan, in the year 2448 (1313 BCE), God delivered the Jewish people, who numbered at that time some several million, from Egyptian slavery (commemorated today by the holiday of Passover) through their leader Moses.

For forty-nine days, the Jews traveled in the wilderness until they came to the foot of Mount Sinai. On the 6th of the Hebrew month of Sivan, God revealed Himself to the entire Jewish nation and gave them the Ten Commandments, along with the complete Torah. (This event is commemorated today by the holiday of Shavuot.) Moses then spent forty days on Mount Sinai receiving all of the Torah's details, instructions, and explanations.

At that historic time, the Jewish nation accepted the responsibility to uphold and live by the Torah's laws and they modified their lifestyles accordingly.

The Torah itself became known as the Written Torah, or Written Law, while the explanations became known as the Oral Torah, or Oral Law.

We need the Oral Torah in order to understand many of the 613 mitzvot. For example, the Torah commands men to don *Tefillin* (phylacteries) each weekday when reciting the morning prayers, yet the Written Torah does not state what they look like, how they should be made, or when they should be worn. Similarly, in the Torah God commands Moses to slaughter kosher animals *"as I have commanded you,"* yet the Written Torah never describes this method.

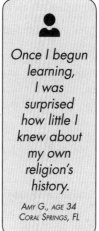

Once I begun learning, I was surprised how little I knew about my own religion's history.

AMY G., AGE 34
CORAL SPRINGS, FL

That information was taught by Moses who entrusted this "Oral tradition" to the Elders, Rabbis, and Judges. They, in turn, were responsible for teaching it to the Jewish people, to whom God commanded, *"You should act in accordance with the teachings that they instruct you"* (Deuteronomy 17:10).

The Oral Torah was later written down and recorded in the *Talmud* and Code of Jewish Law (*Shulchan Aruch*). Both have been passed down intact and are readily available for study.

ALL JEWS RECEIVED THE TORAH

According to the *Midrash* (classical Rabbinic Biblical interpretation), every Jewish soul that ever existed and that ever will come into the world witnessed the Giving of the Torah at Mount Sinai, and committed to following the Torah's commandments.

The account of the "Giving of the Torah" by God and the acceptance of its law as taught by Moses by the entire Jewish People was recounted not just by a single group of people, but by the millions of Jewish people who experienced it firsthand:

people of different mentalities and intellectual abilities, people with different backgrounds and interests. They all charged their children to follow the same path, who in turn, passed it on to their children, often under the most trying circumstances, without interruption until our times.

The descendants of the Jews who personally witnessed the Giving of the Torah later spread out across the globe due to exploration, commerce, or exile. They recounted and attested to the same events, including all the mitzvot, many thousands of years later. Indeed, throughout history, millions of Jews have always known that the Torah and all its laws exactly as we know and practice them today were given by God at Mount Sinai. With determination they maintained the authenticity of the way the Torah was taught and practiced. Today, we follow the exact same tradition based upon this uninterrupted chain of active and involved Jews.

Once I started keeping kosher, I found it elevated my entire life.

CARL L., AGE 57
NEW YORK, NY

THE TORAH: BLUEPRINT OF CREATION

Our Sages declared, *"God looked into the Torah to create the world"* (*Zohar, Terumah, 161b*). This means that the Torah preceded the world and was the sole force and reason for its creation. Through our living by the Torah, Godliness is drawn into every facet of the world, bringing it to its perfection. Thus, the Torah is not merely concerned with "high matters" such as morality and ethics, but also simple, mundane activities such as eating and drinking — one's *total* life experience. Therefore, in order to live fully and completely, one looks to the Torah for instruction and guidance. It's the world's "Owner's Manual," written by its very own Designer and Creator.

HIGHER LIVING

With the giving of the Torah, God bestowed upon the Jewish people a legacy of higher living so that we are able to identify our will with that of our Creator. The laws of the Torah guide this alignment in every phase of our lives: from the foods we eat to the clothing we wear; from the way we raise crops to the way we conduct business. This enables us to be a "holy people," by both serving as an example of Godly living and by bringing goodness and Godliness into the world.

In essence, God empowers us as Jews to sanctify what would otherwise be plain, mundane, or even base, physical activities. Indeed, unlike philosophies or religions that shun all things physical, Judaism enthusiastically embraces all of life's experiences and provides a well-defined path to elevate it.

SPIRITUALIZING THE MATERIAL

According to Judaism, man is the Divine instrument to make this world a fitting abode of Godliness in which both man and God can be in complete harmony. In this context, creation is seen as a process leading from God to man by materializing the spiritual; fulfillment is seen as the process leading from man to God by man's spiritualizing the material. When we use something physical to do a mitzvah, we separate it from its mundane state and transform it into something higher, something Godly, something that exists to serve God. Something like you.

The kosher dietary laws, for example, demonstrate that two people can be eating food, both tasting the same thing, and yet be on completely different spiritual planes — one is engaged in a purely physical act while the other a more, spiritual one.

MITZVAH MEANS CONNECTION

The word *mitzvah* is commonly translated from Hebrew as "commandment." However, mitzvah also means "fusing" and "connection." The mitzvot of the Torah are God's invitations for us to connect to Him. When the mitzvot are performed faithfully and precisely as specified in the Torah, they become the pathways through which we build and maintain this relationship. On a deeper level, being infinite, God is everywhere. Following the Torah's mitzvot connects us to this Infinite Light, causing it to permeate the world with God's Infinite goodness and, with time, enabling us to spiritually elevate ourselves too.

EMBRACING THE "TOTAL LIFE EXPERIENCE"

The fact is that mitzvot such as keeping kosher allow the Jew to connect to God not only while praying or meditating, or while standing in a holy place such as a synagogue, but at home, at work, and everywhere in between — even as often as he craves food.

If God is everywhere, then it makes sense that there is a way for me to experience Him in all places.

JAMIE P., AGE 17
LIVINGSTON, NJ

A cynic once derided Jewish law because it pervades every aspect of daily life, even the seemingly base and mundane. He asked rhetorically, "Why would an infinite and omniscient God possibly need such detailed service?" A more knowledgeable friend replied, "You have things reversed. Judaism is the only religion that provides the means to sanctify one's entire life experiences — from the most mundane to the most profound. This sanctification is possible not just one day a week or once a day, but at all times and in all places — for God is found everywhere. By following the Torah, the Jew has considerably more opportunities to experience God in both time and space, body and soul. If you were sensitive, instead of deriding the Jewish way of life, you would be jealous of it!"

DOES GOD REALLY CARE WHAT I EAT?

Yes. God wants us to be healthy both physically and spiritually, and the kosher dietary laws are definitely a part of that picture. In fact, the classical Sage Maimonides writes that foods forbidden by the Torah are indeed unwholesome and unhealthy.

However, health alone is not the reason we keep kosher. The kosher dietary laws show us how to choose between foods that refine, and foods that degrade our temperaments. Since our soul is from God, He knows best how to nourish it.

We keep kosher because it is a commandment in the Torah. It is about our essential needs as a Jew. Furthermore, God wants to reward us for fulfilling His commandments, and for helping make the world a welcoming abode for God's Presence.

KOSHER AS A REMINDER ABOUT GOD

We think about food more often than we realize. Food is a necessity for life like air and water. Few activities take up as much of our time or evoke as much emotion as food. Indeed, every few hours we embark on a mission to search for food or drink to stave off our hunger and thirst and replenish our energies. If we pause and think, our continuous encounter with hunger reminds us how vulnerable our existence is, and how dependant we truly are on something outside ourselves. By observing the kosher dietary laws, the same hunger that reflects the frailty of our lives acts as a reminder of God, the true Giver of Life.

BEING GRATEFUL FOR MITZVOT

An old (but misguided) saying goes, "One mitzvah can change the world; two will make you tired." As funny (and irreverent) as it sounds, this feeling rings true for many who mistakenly believe that following the Torah fully and completely can be a tremendous burden, God forbid. In truth, the way we feel about anything we do is a matter of the way we view it in our own minds and hearts.

There is a parable that explains this point very well.

A little dove is standing near the ocean's edge, raising her voice heavenwards, and crying that she cannot outrun the animals that want to devour her. God listens and assures her that He will do something to help.

The next morning, the dove awakens to find two appendages attached to her back. She excitedly hurries along, eagerly willing her frail legs to move faster and faster along the ground. Yet she finds that not only can't she run, she is even more restrained by all this extra weight!

She cries out again in despair, "Lord, this is help? Not only does Your solution not make my life easier – it's ten times worse than before!"

God soothes her, saying, "My little bird, these 'heavy attachments' are wings. If you train yourself to use them, you will be able to escape the limitation of being on the ground and soar towards the sky. Then again, you can also sit on your legs and complain how burdensome the wings are. The choice is yours!"

> *"Blessed are You, Lord our God, King of the universe, who has chosen us from among all the nations and given us His Torah. Blessed are You Lord, Who gives the Torah."*

You've just read the blessing all Jews recite before reading from the Torah. Why did the Sages formulate the blessing in this manner? You can probably guess: as Jews, we feel *lucky* and are *grateful* to God for giving us His mitzvot and sharing His wisdom with us. In other words, how fortunate are we for the privilege to live our lives and to raise our families in emulation of God's ways.

As mentioned earlier, Mitzvot, or for that matter all Jewish religious practices, are not about separation or deprivation, but are part of creating a joyous life of connection to God. Taking on the mitzvah of kosher observance is a wonderful step in that direction, and hopefully a stepping stone for bringing more holiness into your life, with the addition and performance of many other mitzvot.

KOSHER IN THE TORAH

The Torah groups all animal creatures into four categories: those that live on land, in the air, in the sea, and insects. Quite a few verses in the Torah list those that a Jew is permitted or not permitted to eat. Other verses describe the laws of separation of meat from dairy foods, inform us of the proper way to prepare kosher animals before they may be eaten, and explain how to make vessels kosher. (All of these will be addressed in more detail in the coming chapters.)

1) EATING ONLY CERTAIN ANIMALS

"Any animal that has a cloven hoof that is completely split into double hooves, and which brings up its cud, you may eat. But these you shall not eat among those that [only] bring up the cud and those that [only] have a cloven hoof." (Leviticus 11:4-5)

2) EATING OR BENEFITING FROM THE COMBINATION OF MEAT & MILK

"You shall not cook a young animal in its mother's milk." (Exodus 34:26)

3) EATING ONLY CERTAIN FISH & SEAFOOD

"Among all that are in the water, you may eat these: Any in the water that has fins and scales, those you may eat, whether in the seas or in the rivers. But any that do not have fins and scales, whether in the seas or in the rivers, among all the creeping creatures in the water and among all living creatures that live in the water, are an abomination for you. And they shall be an abomination for you. You shall not eat of their flesh, and their dead bodies you shall hold in abomination. Any that does not have fins and scales in the water is an abomination for you." (Leviticus 11:9-12)

4) EATING ONLY CERTAIN BIRDS & FOWL

"And among birds, you shall hold these in abomination; they shall not be eaten; they are an abomination: the eagle [or the griffin vulture], the kite, the osprey, the kestrel, and the vulture after its species, and the raven after its species, the ostrich, the jay, and the sparrow hawk, and the goshawk after its species; the owl, the gull, the little owl; the bat, the starling, the magpie; the stork, the heron after its species; the hoopoe and the atalef." (Leviticus 11:14-19)

5) NOT EATING AN ANIMAL THAT WAS TORN APART, AND BY EXTENSION, ANY ANIMAL THAT IS MORTALLY ILL

"You shall be holy people to Me; flesh torn in the field you shall not eat." (Exodus 22:30)

6) KOSHER SLAUGHTER

"You may eat from your cattle or sheep, which God has given to you, provided that you first slaughter them as I have commanded you." (Deuteronomy 12:21)

7) NOT EATING BLOOD & CERTAIN FATS OF KOSHER ANIMALS

"You shall not eat any forbidden fat or blood." (Leviticus 3:17)

8) NOT EATING WORMS, INSECTS, OR CREEPING ANIMALS

"Any creeping creature that creeps on the ground is an abomination; it shall not be eaten." (Leviticus 11:41)

"And this is unclean for you among creeping creatures that creep on the ground: the weasel, the mouse, and the toad after its species; the hedgehog, the chameleon, the lizard, the snail, and the mole." (Leviticus 11:29-30)

9) NOT EATING FLYING INSECTS

"Any flying insect that walks on four is an abomination for you." (Leviticus 11:21-29)

10) KOSHERIZING & IMMERSION OF VESSELS IN A MIKVAH

"The gold, the silver, the copper, the iron, the tin, and the lead...you shall pass through the fire...and be cleansed with the sprinkling waters of the mikvah (body of living waters)." (Numbers 31:22-23)

TODAY'S ACTION
Become aware
of the spiritual
aspects of eating
food.

DAY 2

The Spiritual Side
of Kosher

*I*nterestingly, the kosher dietary laws appear in the same Torah section that deals with holiness and sanctification. One verse reads, *"And you shall sanctify yourselves and be holy, because I [God] am holy"* (Leviticus 11:44). Yet one would not usually think that food, which is physical, goes together with holiness, which is ethereal. By placing the two concepts in such proximity, the Torah suggests that a connection between them does in fact exist: holiness is to be found in ordinary, physical things as anywhere else. The noted Biblical commentator *Rashi* explains that the term "holy" also implies self-restraint. In this context, being holy means being in control of oneself. Mastery over oneself is the path that leads to holiness. The ability to practice restraint frees the person from the grip of his natural impulses and bestows true individual freedom — a life of true holiness.

THE "GOD PARTICLE"

To better understand how something physical like food can impact the spiritual, our Sages quote the verse that was presented earlier, *"Man does not live by bread alone, but by the word of God"* (Deuteronomy 8:3). They explain this to mean that it is not food alone that bestows life, but the "life-sustaining" spark of Godliness that is embedded in it. To better understand this phrase, let's explore some *Kabbalistic* (Jewish mystical teachings) concepts relating to the creation of the world in general, and the creation of food in particular.

If we study the account of Creation as related in the Torah (Genesis 1:1-31), we notice that on each of the six days the verse states, *"And God said..."* (followed by *"'Let there be light'... 'Let there be an expanse in the midst of the water'... 'Let the earth sprout vegetation'..."* etc.) to enact the process of creation.

Our Sages explain that each of the 22 letters of the Hebrew alphabet contains a unique Godly life-force, and by combining them in specific forms, God "produces" certain results. This is not dissimilar to the process of combining elements in chemistry. Thus, for example, when God uses the word *"OHR"* (אור), which is a combination of the unique mystical qualities of the Hebrew letters "א" (Alef), "ו" (Vav), and "ר" (Reish), the ability for "light" to exist is brought into the world. This utterance continues to sustain light's vitality until the time God chooses to withdraw His energy.

The same applies to the rest of creation. Every single physical thing — from the biggest planet down to the tiniest sub-atomic particle — contains a Godly spark that serves as its life-force; without this Godly energy it will cease to exist.

Therefore, when one eats bread, for example, its bulk, fiber, and nutrients serve mainly as a vehicle to introduce its inherent "Godly spark" and life-force to the Godly soul of the person. The soul absorbs and is nourished by this Godly spark, sustaining the body with its spiritual Godly elements. The rest of the actual physical material passes through the body and eventually returns to the earth, only to begin the process again.

With this in mind, we may now recognize how certain foods are positive and "healthy" for the soul, while others are negative or "toxic" for the soul. Just as unhealthy foods can clog up the body's arteries and lead to disease, so too does non-kosher food gum up the spiritual frequencies connecting the soul to the body, inhibiting the Jewish soul from expressing itself through it.

From this perspective, the forbidden foods and food combinations listed in the Torah contain negative spiritual potentials that, when consumed, distort the Jewish soul's spiritual sensitivity.

ELEVATING THE NATURAL ORDER

Yet there's more to keeping kosher than just taking care of ourselves. In Jewish mystical teachings, we learn of four main categories of physical existence. If any were to cease performing their natural tasks, the world would collapse.

They are (in ascending order of importance):

1) *Domaim* - Hebrew for "inanimate"; this includes sand, stones, rocks, etc.

2) *Tzomayach* - Hebrew for "vegetation"; this includes grass, flowers, trees, etc.

3) *Chai* - Hebrew for "living"; this includes the entire animal kingdom.

4) *Medaber* - Hebrew for "speaking"; the category for intelligent human beings.

DOMAIM, even though it is mostly inert and still, serves as a crucial component of the life of tzomayach. Remove a tree or plant from the earth and it will die. In simple terms, domaim supports the life of tzomayach.

I never realized that the Judaism I grew up with had such depth and meaning.

TIBOR W., AGE 29
DETROIT, MI

TZOMAYACH, a step up from domaim (since it can bloom and bear seeds and fruit, whereas domaim cannot) supports the life of animals that make up the category of life known as chai. Most animals are herbivores and depend on vegetation for nourishment. Yet tzomayach is still bound to the earth and does not have freedom of movement.

CHAI, a step up from tzomayach (since it can live detached from the earth), serves as a component in the life of medaber, which obtains physical assistance and nourishment from it. Yet chai does not have free choice, human intelligence, nor the gift of speech.

MEDABER, the peak in the ascending order, is the extreme opposite of the inanimate state of domaim; nor must it remain attached to the earth as tzomayach, or imprisoned by instinct as the animal kingdom of chai. Yet it is sustained and nourished by all three.

Kabbalah teaches that this upward progression doesn't stop with the medaber. Mankind's duty is to complete the entire cycle of creation, elevating the energy derived from the lower three domains by using it in the service of God.

Even though I don't consider myself fully observant yet, I always felt that when doing mitzvot, I should do them with energy derived from kosher food.

ANNA W., AGE 52
MACON, GA

For example, when a Jewish person makes the appropriate blessing and eats kosher food, and with the energy derived from the food he does a *mitzvah* (commandment) from the Torah, he elevates not only himself but the domaim, tzomayach, and chai. He is enabling the entire order of creation to "return to its Source" in a more refined state than when it started. In essence, the medaber enables all of creation to soar higher than any individual component of the natural order can do individually.

MAKING YOUR MITZVOT COUNT

Finally, as the essences and spiritual energies of non-kosher food are dissonant with the Jewish soul, mitzvot performed with their energies remain "trapped" from ascending on High and do not purify the world spiritually. Jews must therefore be very careful to eat only kosher food so that the mitzvot they perform will freely bind with God's light and achieve their fullest expression.

BEING A PARTNER IN CREATION

The bottom line: The Jew has a role to play in the ongoing creation of the world. His role affects not only himself, his family, and his community, but the very earth itself. By living in accordance with the Torah, the Jew is elevating the mundane and completing the order of creation, becoming an actual partner with God. Eating kosher is a significant component of that crucial progression.

Talk about global responsibility!

TODAY'S ACTION
Get in touch
with a relative
or friend who
observes kosher.

DAY 3

3,300 Years
of Kosher Living

*F*rom the very moment that Moses taught the Jewish people the kosher dietary laws, keeping kosher has become a way of life for all Jews. What's more, Jews have always taken pride in these laws and found satisfaction in upholding them. Jewish history books are overflowing with stories of our ancestors' determination to uphold their commitment to kosher, even under the most challenging circumstances. Indeed, there were many periods in our long and varied history when keeping kosher

My grandfather told me how he had to observe kosher in secret, otherwise he would have been persecuted.

TOVA H., AGE 31
FLATBUSH, NY

was considered a national "crime," especially under the Greeks, during the Spanish Inquisition, and, more recently, under the Communist regime in Russia. These despotic regimes understood that destroying the ability to keep kosher was the first step in obliterating Jewish life, God forbid. Yet despite the harsh edicts and threats, many Jews held steadfast to kosher (and, for that matter, all the *mitzvot* [commandments] in the Torah). We survived all our enemies and are here today because of those heroes.

THE FIRST KOSHER-KEEPERS

When the Jewish people were taught the kosher dietary laws by Moses at Mount Sinai, they were eager to implement them immediately. In fact, we recall their zeal on the Jewish holiday of Shavuot, commemorating the giving of the Torah at Mount Sinai. During this holiday, it is customary to serve a dairy meal, the story of which is fascinating.

Tradition tells us that when the Jews learned the kosher dietary laws, they realized that before their utensils could be used for food, they needed to be kosherized to remove the non-kosher impurities and flavors absorbed in them. Until each family managed to do this, they ate only dairy foods which didn't involve a great deal of preparation, thus requiring the use of non-kosher utensils. We eat a dairy meal on Shavuot, thousands of years later, to recall our ancestors' simple faith and willingness to follow God's directives perfectly and completely, and without delay.

WORKING HARD TO UPHOLD KOSHER

.Only a few generations ago, food preparation was a private affair, something each family did for itself. Part of the skill of running a household included the knowledge of turning raw foods into delicious and nourishing kosher meals. Industrial factories churning out thousands of kosher food products were a distant dream. Milk, cheeses, and butter were obtained from one's cow or local dairy farm; chicken and cattle were raised at home or bought at a live market.

To demonstrate some of the hardships our great-grandparents endured to keep kosher, let us compare the amount of dedication and preparation needed to prepare kosher chicken in the past, with what it takes today.

CHICKEN FOR DINNER — BEFORE TODAY

Go into the yard or market and find a good, healthy-looking chicken. Head over to the home of the local *shochet*, a religious Jew proficient in the kosher dietary laws of ritual slaughter. Wait your turn, then hand him the chicken. Afterwards, take the chicken and begin plucking the feathers. When you're done, open the chicken and inspect the organs to make sure they appear healthy (you learned what to look for from your mother). Then soak the chicken in a container of water, after which you thoroughly salt each part with coarse salt and let it stand, allowing the blood (which is not kosher) to drain. Following this, you will rinse the chicken and soak it again.

My grand-parents kept kosher, but for some reason in our home we never did. I want to correct that for our children.

MARK W., AGE 42
CINCINNATI, OH

41

Finally, if there are no complications or *shailos* ("questions," inquiries, or points requiring clarification to ensure they conform to Jewish dietary law) to pose to a kosher expert, the chicken is ready for cooking and serving.

CHICKEN FOR DINNER — TODAY

Stop by your local kosher butcher, kosher market, or any supermarket with a pre-packaged kosher meat section, and pick up a pre-kosherized quartered chicken. Season. Put it in the oven. Serve. Collect compliments. (It's really that easy!)

Now you can understand the incredulous look some elderly Jews will give when they hear young people groan about how "difficult" it is to keep kosher nowadays!

KOSHER IN THE "NEW WORLD"

As early as the 1600s, kosher meat was already sold commercially in America. Around the 1900s, mass kosher food production began to take root, thanks to the pioneering efforts of Jewish entrepreneurs such as Manischewitz and Rokeach.

With the rapid industrialization of food production and the introduction of modern food preparation techniques, the need to have kosher dietary law experts oversee and regulate the process arose (see "Day 17"). Thus, around 1924, the Orthodox Union established a kosher-certifying agency, later to become known as the "OU." This development helped ensure that food labeled as kosher and bore an "OU" symbol on the packaging was indeed so.

Around 1935, a second agency called the "OK" was established to serve the growing demands of the marketplace. Together, these two agencies are responsible for many of the kosher products we see on supermarket shelves today. There are also many other kosher-certifying agencies helping to make keeping kosher easier than ever before.

Today, most supermarkets carry literally thousands of quality food products that are certified kosher. Indeed, the kosher industry is booming today like at no other time in history.

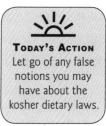

TODAY'S ACTION
Let go of any false
notions you may
have about the
kosher dietary laws.

DAY 4

For the Record:
Common Misconceptions

 $\mathcal{O}$ ne of the first things to do upon embarking on the journey to keeping kosher, is to separate fact from fiction. Misinformation about kosher observance is very prevalent, even though all the kosher dietary laws originate from the Torah and are fully and clearly explained in the *Code of Jewish Law*. It should therefore be fairly easy to trim the fat from the meat, so to say, for all one has to do is study the sources to learn what is true and what is a *bubbe maase*, a "grandmother's tale." However, for those who lack a command of the Hebrew language, this is easier said than done. But do not despair! Today we'll set the record straight for many common misconceptions once and for all.

MISCONCEPTION #1

KOSHER MEANS "CLEAN." IN BIBLICAL TIMES OUR ANCESTORS HAD NO REFRIGERATION SO THE KOSHER DIETARY LAWS WERE INVENTED TO PROTECT PEOPLE FROM DISEASE. TODAY, WITH MODERN, SOPHISTICATED TECHNOLOGY, PLUS STRICT GOVERNMENT REGULATION, IT IS NO LONGER NECESSARY TO "OBSERVE KOSHER."

It wasn't until I actually sat down and studied the origin of kosher that I realized how poor my Jewish education was.

MARVIN H., AGE 42
SANTA ROSA, CA

Kosher is a Hebrew word that means "fit" or "proper" — it does not mean clean (even though kosher food tends to be clean too). One could serve a clean piece of ham on sterilized plates, yet the ham remains totally *non-kosher*. The same would be true for "organically raised" pork steak. This is because the Torah spells out quite clearly, *"these"* are the animals, fish, or fowl you may eat, and *"these"* you should not. Nothing to do with cleanliness.

Contrary to popular myth, no direct reason is given in the Torah for the *mitzvah* (commandment) of kosher, other than that it is God's Will, even though we may conjure up many good and rational reasons by using our own intellects. For example, it is true that one can find a thread of cleanliness and purity in the kosher dietary laws.

Furthermore, it is also true that it is probably healthier to do without eating snakes, frogs, insects, pigs, or worms. But physical health benefits alone are not the basis for kosher observance. As we mentioned earlier, Jews observe the kosher dietary laws for the same reason we follow all the other laws of the Torah: because God commanded us so. Since as Jews we believe that the entire Torah is the word of God, we don't pick or choose which laws to observe. As God stated quite clearly in the Torah, *"Do not add to the word which I command you, nor diminish from it"* (Deuteronomy 4:2). The kosher dietary laws in their entirety are immutable, standing for all time.

MISCONCEPTION #2

KEEPING KOSHER LIMITS MY FOOD CHOICES, I'LL GO HUNGRY MOST OF THE TIME.

The average U.S. supermarket is likely to carry some 25,000 items that have kosher symbols on their packaging indicating that they have reliable kosher certification, and not just items in the "Ethnic/Kosher" aisle. Some may even have as many as 50,000 kosher items, and each year approximately 2,500 new kosher food items are introduced to the market. So choices abound!

Later on (see "Day 17"), we will learn about many different kosher symbols and how to spot them. For now, to assure ourselves that we'll not go hungry while keeping kosher, let us go on an imaginary visit to a kosher-observant home and see what kind of kosher foods are in the kitchen.

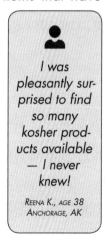

I was pleasantly surprised to find so many kosher products available — I never knew!

REENA K., AGE 38
ANCHORAGE, AK

You'll find fruits and vegetables, breads, rolls, and all kinds of delicious baked goods. In the fridge you can find chicken, turkey, ground beef, steaks, roasts or deli-meats. Many types of fish, including salmon, tilapia, Chilean sea bass, flounder, trout, tuna, whitefish and herring might also be there. Keep looking and you'll see whole and low-fat milk, all types of kosher soft and hard cheeses, butter and creams. In the pantry you will find all kinds of cereals, canned vegetables, spices, flavored bread crumbs, wafers, cookies, chips, dips — the list goes on and on.

True, keeping kosher means being aware of what you are buying and eating, but thanks to the ever expanding market for kosher products, you will never go hungry for lack of food, maybe only for a lack of good planning!

MISCONCEPTION #3
THE KOSHER DIETARY LAWS MAY HAVE APPLIED THOUSANDS OF YEARS AGO, BUT IN THE 21ST CENTURY THEY ARE OBSOLETE & IRRELEVANT.

See Misconception #1.

MISCONCEPTION #4
"KOSHER STYLE" IS THE SAME AS REAL KOSHER.

A sign that says "Kosher Style" is usually more about the style than about kosher and cannot be relied upon alone. At most, the food may be similar in presentation or flavor to kosher food recipes, but unless the food is certified as kosher by a reputable kosher certification agency, as evidenced by the display of a current, valid kosher certificate from a recognized kosher certification agency, all similarities to real kosher food end.

Unfortunately, numerous food establishments unwillingly (or even willingly) mislead customers into believing that they are being served kosher food when they are not. Aside from the moral issues involved, this practice is actually illegal. Many states in the U.S. have strict laws against advertising kosher food as kosher when it is not. When it comes to kosher, remember, it's not just about style, it's about substance!

It took me years to realize that my poor Jewish education was no excuse for ignoring my heritage.

MARCELLA L., AGE 46
MIAMI, FL

MISCONCEPTION #5

KOSHER IS FOR ORTHODOX JEWS. I'M NOT RELIGIOUS, SO I DON'T HAVE TO KEEP KOSHER.

Every Jew, regardless of his or her current level of Jewish awareness or observance, has a Jewish soul and is required to fulfill the *mitzvot* (commandments) of the Torah. Keeping kosher is, therefore, just as incumbent on him or her as any of the Torah's other laws, such as observing the Shabbat, giving *tzedakah* (charity), upholding the laws of justice, and so on. It is the way that God wants His children, the Children of Israel, to live their lives.

In fact, the Torah speaks to each individual Jew. For example, the Ten Commandments begin with *"Anochi Hashem Elokecha…,"* which translated from Hebrew means "I am God, your God…") (Exodus 20:2). The Hebrew word used for "your God" is the singular form, *Elokecha,* and not *Elokeichem* (plural), teaching us that God addresses each and every individual personally and directly. Thus each and every Jew carries his or her own personal obligation to follow the mitzvot of the Torah and is imbued with the power to do so.

Of course the Torah realizes that people are also the product of their environments. Therefore, if a Jew grew up without any substantive Jewish education, while he or she is still obligated to observe all of the Torah's laws, there is room for the individual process that includes a gradual — but steady — embracing of the mitzvot, but no Jew is ever exempt from their obligation to follow the Torah meticulously.

MISCONCEPTION #6

KEEPING KOSHER IS VERY EXPENSIVE.

This really depends on what you like to eat! All kidding aside, this misconception is only partially true. Manufacturers do have to add in the extra cost of doing a "kosher run." Depending on the product, they may have to obtain exclusively kosher ingredients, reformulate current recipes, and stop production lines in order to kosherize the equipment. They also have the added expense of obtaining reliable kosher certification which will guide and supervise the entire production process. All this can add between ten to fifteen percent to the cost of a product (mainly meat and dairy products). But by far, the vast majority of kosher foods available today cost nearly the same as non-kosher ones.

The fact is, all fresh fruits and vegetables, unprocessed grains and nuts, kosher breads, and the many thousands of common pantry items on supermarket shelves that display a kosher symbol on their package are priced fairly. So *ess gezunt* (that's Yiddish for hearty appetite)!

MISCONCEPTION #7

"KOSHER" MEANS THE FOOD WAS BLESSED BY A RABBI.

When a company wishes to obtain kosher certification, it hires a Rabbi who is an expert in the kosher dietary laws to advise them and supervise the entire food production effort, making sure the ingredients, equipment, and end-product are completely kosher. Perhaps workers seeing a Rabbi roaming the plant during production think he is merely "blessing the food."

True, the relationship of blessings to kosher food is not totally alien to Judaism, for it is indeed a mitzvah for Jews to recite a short blessing of thanks to God before and another after eating or drinking any kosher food or beverage (see "Day 15"). Nevertheless, the bottom line is that a blessing has nothing to do with making a food kosher. As mentioned above, kosher means "fit" or "proper." Either the food meets the requirements of the kosher dietary laws or it does not. Blessing or praying doesn't change the kosher status of any food any more than waving an apple up and down will turn it into an orange.

MISCONCEPTION #8

I'M A VEGETARIAN. I DON'T EAT MEAT OR DAIRY PRODUCTS, SO I DON'T HAVE TO BE CONCERNED IF THE FOOD IS KOSHER OR NOT.

Kosher doesn't only pertain to meat and dairy. Any food can be rendered non-kosher if it was prepared on or with equipment that was used for non-kosher food, or contains non-kosher ingredients. For example, a freshly tossed salad can be just as non-kosher as a piece of ham. How? If, for example, the oil used to dress the salad was derived from, or produced on, the same equipment as non-kosher animal fat, the entire salad would now be non-kosher.

Even seemingly innocuous spices and food colorings can contain "harmless" additives and preservatives that are actually derived from non-kosher sources (i.e., bugs, beetles, etc.).

The same rule applies to cooked foods free of any additives or spices whatsoever; and cut or diced raw fruits and vegetables. This is because the moment food is cooked in a non-kosher pot or oven, or prepared with non-kosher utensils, it inherits the non-kosher status and become non-kosher (with several minor exceptions).

Nothing made sense until I understood the basic foundations of kosher law — then it all became clear.

MARK E., AGE 30
ANN ARBOR, MI

MISCONCEPTION #9

IT'S OKAY TO EAT A SALAD AT A NON-KOSHER OR VEGETARIAN RESTAURANT.

It is laudable when people try to make kosher food choices when eating out. While this is a step in the right direction, one has to really know what's kosher and what's not before thinking he or she is really "eating kosher."

First, a cardinal rule of kosher: any "neutrally kosher" food may be rendered non-kosher by contamination with non-kosher foods during preparation or serving. In the above case we have three kosher problems. One, the utensils used to prepare the salad aren't kosher, as they are also used for non-kosher foods; two, the kosher status of the vegetable oil, vinegar, flavorings, or additives that are added are unknown; and three, the lettuce was not checked for insects which are extremely prevalent in leafy vegetables and are just as non-kosher as ham (actually worse, because eating insects violates more Biblical laws than eating ham).

Therefore, when the same utensils used to prepare and serve non-kosher food are used for what may be "naturally" kosher products (i.e., raw vegetables), the food can be rendered non-kosher and a Jew may not eat them. As we'll learn later (see "Day 13"), utensils that are used for non-kosher food must first be properly cleaned and expertly purged ("kosherized") of all non-kosher flavor before they can be used for kosher food.

Finally, even if not eating any "problem foods," or anything at all (for example, attending a meeting at a non-kosher food establishment but not eating there), there is the issue of *"Maarat Ayin,"* which is Hebrew for "creating an appearance of wrong-doing." Another Jew seeing you in a non-kosher restaurant may think the establishment is kosher and will be misled to eat non-kosher food there because of you. He is unaware of your personal precautions, or that you just went in for a meeting or a glass of water, etc. And as Jews, we have a spiritual as well as a social responsibility for one another.

MISCONCEPTION #10

MOST OF THE TORAH & TALMUDIC LAWS WE HAVE TODAY, INCLUDING THE KOSHER DIETARY LAWS, WERE INVENTED BY VARIOUS RABBIS OVER THE COURSE OF HISTORY, OR ARE DISTORTED FROM THEIR ORIGINAL INTENT DUE TO FAULTY TRANSMISSION OVER SO MANY GENERATIONS.

This misconception is similar to the "broken phone" argument, which goes something like this: if you have ten people stand in a row and whisper a message in the ear of the first person telling him to relay it to the next person, and he to the next, all the way down the line, chances are good that the message will come out at the other end distorted, if not completely wrong. Thus, it is argued, it is conceivable that the Torah we follow today, some 3,300 years after it was given, is not the same one given to Moses at Mount Sinai, God forbid.

According to this theory, a Torah scroll from Yemen should differ significantly from a Torah scroll from a Chicago synagogue; or a Talmud from Babylonia should be markedly different than one from Poland due to the passage of time, human errors, and so on. However, history has shown that this is simply not the case.

Let's borrow the above "broken phone" argument to explain. Instead of having just one row of ten people, we'll line up fifty rows (that's 500 people) and give the first person in each row the same message. What are the chances that the message delivered by the last person across all fifty rows will be the same? Less than zero, right? Based on the above theory, each row should provide a different result. If the last person in each row were to report the complete message exactly as relayed to the first person, you'd say it was impossible, if not an open miracle.

We are fortunate to live in a time when the world has become a "smaller place," and people from all continents across the globe are able to meet and communicate like never before in history. This is a good time to put the theory to the test! And what do we find? That the Torah and Talmud we study today are fully identical to those found across the globe. In every country and continent they are exact *to the letter.*

Communities in the Diaspora that were completely cut off from the bulk of the Jewish people for close to 2,000 years (such as in Yemen), have the same exact Torah and *Talmud* as are studied around the world today.

So, be assured that the Torah studied and practiced by observant Jews today is the same as the one given to Moses at Mount Sinai 3,300 years ago.

DAY 5

Basic Kosher
Concepts

*B*efore exploring some general concepts of kosher, let's review three central principals. First, Jews observe kosher because God, the Creator of the world, has commanded us to do so in the Torah. Even though there may be numerous compelling "rational" reasons to observe kosher, ultimately it is observed simply because it is the Will of God. Second, kosher observance affects in a profound way not only the body but also the Jewish soul. As discussed earlier (see "Day 2"), we become what we eat. Third, if any component of an item is not kosher, the *entire* item can become non-kosher. This particular principal may be better understood by analogy of a peanut allergy. Even if a food has no relation to peanuts but was produced on equipment that once manufactured peanut items, precautions are taken. This is understandable since even trace amounts of peanut in any food can be harmful. The same is true for kosher food that has been prepared on non-kosher equipment or equipment that was not properly kosherized — it can easily become non-kosher.

KOSHER & NON-KOSHER MEAT

Kosher animals have completely split hooves and chew their cud. Animals that exhibit only one (or neither) of those features are not kosher and cannot be eaten by a Jew. Common kosher animals such as cows, sheep, goats, and deer have both of these features, and thus are kosher. Common non-kosher animals that do not have both of these signs include pigs, horses, donkeys, camels, and rabbits.

The Torah states (Leviticus 11:4-8) that only four animals have just one of the kosher signs, and are thus not kosher. These include the pig (only has split-hooves), camel (only chews its cud, and does not have a completely split hoof), hare (only chews its cud), and hyrax (only chews its cud).

Parenthetically, the fact that the Torah explicitly states that only four such animals have one of these signs (no small claim since most of the world was unexplored at that time) is sometimes cited to support the Torah's Divine origin. For, in the 3,300-plus years since the giving of the Torah, not one additional animal with these characteristics has been discovered.

Kosher meat and fowl must be slaughtered and inspected by a *shochet* (expert ritual slaughterer), and then salted to drain their blood before they can be consumed by a Jew. A kosher animal that dies on its own, is killed by another animal, or in any manner other than kosher slaughter, is considered non-kosher and may not be eaten. This even includes kosher animals that have been slaughtered in accordance with Jewish law, but are later found to have diseased organs or broken limbs (which is apparent only after an internal inspection).

I remember learning that just as split hooves keep the animal above the ground, Jews must elevate themselves above the material world.

AVRAHAM J., AGE 67
MUNSTER, IN

KOSHER FOWL & POULTRY

Kosher fowl includes all species that were handed down through reliable Jewish tradition as kosher. Today, these are known to be chicken, turkey, and certain geese and duck. All other species of fowl are considered non-kosher (see "Day 19").

KOSHER SLAUGHTER

The Torah is exceptionally sensitive to the welfare of animals and commands man to be the same. While mankind was given complete dominion over the animal and vegetable kingdoms (Genesis 9:2-4), the Torah legislated many rules for their protection. For example, a Jew is prohibited from feeding himself before his animals (your animals come first!) (*Brachot* 40a); showing cruelty to animals, which also includes hunting for sport (*Bava Metizah* 32); harnessing two different animal species to pull a plow or wagon together (Deuteronomy 22:10), muzzling an ox while it is threshing (Deuteronomy 25:4), and eating the blood or flesh of animals while they're still alive (Genesis 9:4).

In this spirit, the Torah sets strict rules about slaughtering kosher animals and fowl. As mentioned above, the slaughter must be performed by a shochet. He must use an extremely sharp knife (the smallest nick on the blade renders it unfit), and swiftly sever the arteries in the neck of the animal. Severing these arteries renders the animal immediately unconscious, with death instantly following.

After the slaughter, the animal is inspected internally for any disease. If found to be healthy, the meat is then soaked and salted to drain it of its blood (it is Biblically forbidden to consume blood), and certain veins and fats are removed. Only after all these steps are proficiently completed is the meat fit for kosher consumption.

KOSHER FISH

All fish that have fins and scales are kosher. Other sea creatures that have only fins or only scales are not kosher and may not be eaten by Jews (see "Day 21"). Kosher fish must also be prepared using kosher knives and utensils.

Common kosher fish include salmon, tilapia, Chilean sea bass, flounder, trout, tuna, whitefish, and many more. One must see the fins and scales on the fish for it to be considered kosher. For this reason, one cannot buy filleted fish in a fish store or supermarket unless it has reliable kosher certification, as the fins and scales have been removed and one cannot know for certain which specie of fish is being bought.

Shellfish, shrimp, swordfish, eel, lobster, and all other seafood that do not have fins and scales are not kosher, and are forbidden to be eaten by Jews.

FORBIDDEN FOOD COMBINATIONS

According to kosher dietary law, meat and dairy products cannot be cooked or eaten together; they must always be separated. Some Sages propose a mystical explanation that milk, which is known as the "sustenance of life," and meat, which is consumed only after the animal is dead, represent two opposing spiritual forces, life and death, and mixing them creates an undesirable spiritual energy.

Due to health related concerns discussed in the Talmud, fish, too, is not cooked or eaten with meat (but may be served as a separate course in a meaty meal, using separate dishes and silverware). Some pious Jews extend this protective measure to include not eating fish and milk together; however, most *Halachic* (Jewish legal) authorities are lenient in this matter. All authorities agree that, as with eating fish in a meaty meal, it is permissible to eat fish during a dairy meal, provided it is served as a separate course on its own plates and silverware.

WAITING PERIOD BETWEEN EATING MEAT & DAIRY

A period of time must elapse between eating meat and dairy; or dairy and then meat. This is to keep the meat and dairy foods from being mixed in the mouth or digested together.

It is the prevailing custom for adults to wait six hours after eating meat before eating any dairy food (the time it takes for the initial digestion of meat), and one hour between dairy and meat (since most dairy products clear and digest faster than meat). It is also the custom to wait six hours after eating hard cheeses that are aged six months or more (i.e., Parmesan cheese), as they take longer to digest. However, most kosher certified cheeses require only a one hour waiting period.

Children should be trained from an early age to wait between meat and dairy meals and *vice versa*. Children under the age of three do not have to wait a fixed amount between eating meat and dairy foods. They should, however, have their mouth cleaned of any meaty food substance before eating or drinking dairy. (This does not mean that they may eat meat and dairy together.)

Beginning from the age of three, healthy children should be encouraged to wait three hours after eating meat before eating dairy. From the age of six to seven, the time is increased to four hours. At eight, five hours. At nine, six hours (as do adults).

Regarding the time between eating dairy and meat, some are more lenient and suffice with giving the child a dry food (such as a cracker) to clean his or her mouth of any dairy residue. Others observe a minimal amount of waiting time (anywhere from 10 to 30 minutes). Inquire as to the custom of your community.

CREEPING CREATURES

Bugs, insects, snails, and all creeping creatures are not kosher, and are forbidden to be eaten by Jews. This is why one must carefully inspect leafy vegetables and certain grains, flours, and legumes, for insects or worms (see "Day 22").

PAREVE

Nature supplies us generously with our daily dietary needs and the Torah permits us to partake to our heart's content. All raw fruits and vegetables, including unprocessed grains, seeds, nuts, and eggs from kosher species of birds and fish, are inherently kosher and are considered *pareve*, meaning "neutral" (neither meaty nor dairy), and may be eaten together with meat or dairy foods (see "Day 22").

Even when dealing with naturally grown foods, one must make sure it has not been "processed" in any way (i.e., roasted, flavored, fortified with vitamins or preservatives, etc.), for the processing may introduce non-kosher ingredients or elements rendering the "natural" food non-kosher. Therefore, when buying processed natural products, always look for a kosher symbol on the package (see "Day 17").

KOSHER WINE & WHISKEY

Wines and liquors must be certified kosher. Some Halachic authorities permit the use of straight, unflavored whiskeys and vodkas, but check with a kosher expert to verify which brands are permissible without kosher certification. Even though alcohol is a seemingly "natural" product, the additives, clarifiers, emulsifiers, etc., used can often be non-kosher (see "Day 24").

Additionally, the production of wine must be performed solely by observant Jews. This is because throughout history (including nowadays) gentiles would consecrate all wine they came in contact with to their deity, and the Torah forbids deriving benefit from anything made or used for idolatrous purposes. This prohibition was also instituted to guard against inappropriate fraternization between Jews and gentiles (as with foods cooked or baked by a non-Jew [see below]).

AGRICULTURAL PRODUCE FROM THE LAND OF ISRAEL

There are numerous laws in the Torah that relate to agricultural produce grown in the Land of Israel. They include tithing the crops, resting the land during the seventh year, and not harvesting the fruit of young trees before the fourth year. These laws are known in Hebrew as *t'rumah, ma'aser, shmittah,* and *orlah.* By and large, these Biblical obligations must still be practiced today. Therefore, agricultural products exported from the Land of Israel need to have reliable kosher certification verifying that these requirements were met (see "Day 22").

COMMERCIALLY PREPARED FOODS

Most commercially sold cooked, or otherwise processed foods, are to be assumed to be non-kosher unless proven to be otherwise. One reason for this is because nowadays factories commonly use hundreds of ingredients, including chemicals and additives, that come from many unknown suppliers.

Furthermore, companies commonly use the same equipment for manufacturing different food products, including those that are definitely non-kosher. Therefore, all manufactured and processed food products must bear reliable kosher certification as evidenced by a kosher symbol on the package, or for a food establishment, a valid, unexpired kosher certificate.

"KOSHER CONTINUITY"

For food to remain kosher, all ingredients and utensils — including stoves and ovens that are used in preparing the food must be kosher. In this context, "kosher" means that the item was used exclusively (meaning totally, completely, absolutely) with kosher food from the time it was brand-new (or properly kosherized). This is because, as mentioned earlier, kosher food is "hyper-sensitive" to contact with non-kosher items, especially when heat is involved (i.e., cooking, baking, even splattering, etc.).

If contact with non-kosher food occurs, the food, no matter how kosher it was when it started out, can (and usually does) become non-kosher. For example, adding bacon bits to a salad makes the up-to-now kosher salad non-kosher, or heating a kosher knish in the same pan used for heating other non-kosher food makes the knish non-kosher, and so on.

KOSHER SUPERVISION & CERTIFICATION

Many products today bear a kosher symbol such as "OU" or "OK" on their label. This means that the respective kosher certifying agency guarantees that the products are 100 percent kosher. Kosher-conscient consumers should only buy processed food if it has a symbol from a reliable kosher certifying agency on the package (see "Day 17"). As a general rule, before buying any food remember to look for a kosher symbol on the package, or for a food establishment, a valid, unexpired kosher certificate.

KOSHER FOODS PREPARED BY A NON-JEW

Milk, bread and baked goods, including all foods that cannot be eaten in their raw state, must have their preparation supervised by a Jew, and a Jew must have some involvement that is integral to the cooking or baking process (i.e., kindling or adding to the fire in the oven, stirring the pot, etc.).

I found it fascinating that many of the kosher dietary laws are effective at preventing assimilation.

ESTHER G., AGE 57
TWIN CITIES, MN

If a non-Jew cooks or bakes important foods (i.e., foods that are fit to be served at a banquet) that cannot be eaten in the raw state, from beginning to end, the food may not be eaten by a Jew. In most cases the vessels used must be kosherized before they can be used again with kosher food.

Bread and baked goods baked by a non-Jew in a commercial setting (i.e., in a commercial bakery or factory) from beginning to end, using only kosher ingredients and equipment, can be considered kosher. But it is preferable for a Jew to be integrally involved in the baking process (see "Day 23").

These laws were enacted by our Sages to protect against assimilation and as a hedge against Biblically forbidden intermarriage. One rationale given is that food prepared for a Jew by a non-Jew will foster a reciprocal obligation, which, in turn, may promote an unhealthy cycle of closeness and attachment.

THE IMPACT OF HEAT ON KOSHER STATUS

In Jewish law, whenever heat is present or introduced, kosher concerns rise along with the temperature. The general idea is that heat causes or aids the absorption of the flavor of the food into the walls of the containing vessel. This flavor is later expelled the next time the vessel is heated. Thus, a pot used for cooking a beef stew becomes meaty and cannot be used later for a dairy soup, since the embedded "meat" taste and dairy soup will mix (a forbidden combination) and make both the food, the pot, and all utensils used non-kosher.

This is why kosher kitchens have separate utensils, with one set being used exclusively for meat and the other for dairy.

Some heat-related kosher terms are:

- *"Yad Soledet,"* which loosely translated from Hebrew means "too hot to touch or eat." Most kosher authorities agree this is from around 110 degrees Fahrenheit (about 44 degrees Celsius) and higher. Items at this temperature transfer flavors or fats when in contact with other items.

- *"Kli Rishon,"* which in Hebrew means "first vessel" (i.e., a cooking implement that was in direct contact with fire). This refers to the contents in an actively boiling pot. If a kosher-neutral (neither meat nor dairy) item falls into the boiling pot, it immediately inherits the status of the food in the pot. Also, all utensils used in a kli rishon acquire the same status as the pot. Therefore, if a dairy spoon or other utensil is used in a meaty kli rishon, there are serious kosher implications and a kosher expert should be consulted.

- *"Kli Sheini,"* which in Hebrew means "second vessel" (i.e., once removed from fire). This refers to food that has been transferred from a first vessel. As a result, it is considered to have slightly cooled and thus poses fewer kosher issues.

- *"Kli Shlishi,"* which in Hebrew means "third vessel" (i.e., twice removed from fire). In this case, the contents were removed from the first vessel, and then removed again from the second vessel. It is considered to have cooled even more than kli sheini and poses even fewer kosher issues.

SHARP FOODS

Sharp foods, such as onion, hot pepper, garlic, etc., are treated in a similar way as hot foods, since the biting sharpness transfers flavor as well. Thus, if you cut a sharp pareve (kosher-neutral) food (i.e., an onion or radish) with a meaty knife, you cannot use the cut-up onion with dairy food (at least the part that touched the knife).

The same is true in reverse — if you cut the onion with a dairy knife, the cut-up onion cannot be used with anything that contains meat. Neither should it be cooked in meaty pots or pans, as it will transfer the "meaty" or the "dairy" flavor.

SEPARATING KITCHEN UTENSILS

Utensils used for meat cannot be used for dairy, and *vice versa*. If one used meaty utensils for dairy, or *vice versa*, the food and the utensils can become non-kosher, the food itself cannot be eaten (even by a non-Jew), and the utensils must be properly kosherized before they can be used again with kosher food (see "Kosher 911" below).

THE KOSHERIZING PROCESSES

A non-kosher utensil, pot, or oven can be kosherized by cleaning the item thoroughly, not using it for 24 hours, and then heating (purging) it with either boiling water or fire. The intense heat removes the flavor that was absorbed in the walls of the vessel and returns the item to a kosher-neutral (pareve) status.

In general, the method of kosherizing is chosen according to how the vessel or utensil was used. If it was used for cooking, then it is kosherized by immersing it entirely in boiling water. If it was used for baking or roasting, then it is kosherized with fire until it glows red- or white-hot.

Not all materials can be kosherized. In some instances this is because the implements will melt or be destroyed in the process (certain plastics, rubber, delicate glass or china, etc.). In other cases it is because they do not purge easily or at all (i.e., certain knives, composite granite, some ceramics, etc.). Consult a kosher expert to be sure.

Some common kosherizing terms are:

- *"Libun Gamur,"* which loosely translated from Hebrew means "severe heating or purging." Fire is used until the item glows red- or white-hot.

- *"Libun Kal,"* which loosely translated from Hebrew means "less severe heating." Causing the item to reach a temperature higher than when it was normally used (i.e., most household ovens are not used above 400 degrees Fahrenheit [about 205 degrees Celsius], so setting it to 450 degrees [about 232 degrees Celsius] for an hour can be sufficient to kosherize it).

- *"Hagalah,"* in Hebrew, means "purging" or "boiling." Here it is used to refer to immersing the vessel in water that has reached a rolling boil (usually from 212 degrees Fahrenheit [about 100 degrees Celsius] and above).

Note that the laws of kosherizing kitchen equipment and utensils are complex and can be difficult to master, especially for the novice. It is thus highly recommended to ask a kosher expert to do the kosherizing for you — at least until you get the hang of it.

"KOSHER 911"

Sometimes kosher questions arise in the kitchen, especially for beginners. For example, a dairy sponge can be mistakenly used to clean a meaty pot under hot water, or a meaty knife was used to cut a cheese lasagna. What do you do now? You ask a kosher expert! In this case, you set aside the utensils and food involved. Then contact a kosher expert and explain the predicament. He will tell you how to proceed. In the meantime, it is okay to wash the utensils in question in cold water (never hot) until their status is clarified.

Some "forensic details" to have prepared for the kosher expert or Rabbi:
- Was the food meaty or dairy?
- Was the food hot or cold?
- How hot was the food or utensil?
- Was the food sharp or spicy?
- How much food was involved?
- What type of utensil was it (i.e., metal, plastic, glass, etc.)?
- When was the utensil used in the last 24 hours, and with which kind of food?

- How long were the items in question in contact with each other?

There are many circumstances where the situation is not as severe as initially thought. However, it's always best to be sure before non-kosher utensils work their way around the kitchen, making everything non-kosher.

"MAARAT AYIN" — RESPONSIBILITY OF PUBLIC PERCEPTION

As a Jew, it is important to consider the ramifications of our actions in private and, even more so, in public. The Torah speaks strongly against "placing a stumbling block before the blind." The rabbis extended this to mean misleading other Jews who might mistake our actions as a sanction that the activity is permitted according to the Torah. What does this mean in the realm of kosher?

Maarat Ayin sensitivity includes not going into a non-kosher restaurant to attend a meeting, get a drink of water, use the restroom, or to get change for the parking meter, especially if there are other options nearby. If another Jew sees that you've entered the establishment, he may think the restaurant is kosher (or that you're not). Either way, the person is under a mistaken impression.

Keeping kosher enabled me to be more aware of my effect on the world around me.

JACOB H., AGE 16
ALBANY, NY

As another example, serving non-dairy ice cream for a dessert after a meaty meal might lead a guest to think it is okay to eat dairy immediately after meat, since he doesn't know the ice cream is non-dairy. (This also can include serving margarine (which looks like butter), non-dairy creamers, or soy "meat" products in a dairy meal, etc.). Being sensitive to Maarat Ayin will remind you to disclose such facts in advance (such as by displaying the carton or product label showing that it is non-dairy), or avoid such sticky situations altogether.

CHILDREN & KOSHER OBSERVANCE

Children should be taught to keep kosher just as adults. They should be trained to look for a kosher symbol on food packages, and what to do when offered a non-kosher item.

Children should also be trained to wait between meat and dairy meals and *vice versa* from an early age. (See "Waiting Period Between Eating Meat & Dairy" earlier in this chapter, regarding the waiting periods for children.)

IMITATION NON-KOSHER FOOD (CRAB, SHRIMP, ETC.)

Even though the *Talmud* states, *"For every non-kosher food, there exists an equivalently savory kosher counterpart"* (*Chullin* 109b), some people seem unable to contain their curiosity which has given rise to a new market of "imitation" non-kosher food. While the ingredients and production process may indeed be kosher on the highest level, the idea of imitating the very foods the Torah calls an "abomination" seems inappropriate and unholy to many, even though reputable kosher agencies give kosher certification to many of these products.

In truth, one needs to examine one's motivations. There is a marked difference between someone undergoing the process of keeping kosher who finds it difficult to leave certain food memories behind, and someone who has kept kosher all his life and wants to know what it's like to eat non-kosher foods.

When the first entrepreneur brought kosher soy "bacon" bits to a leading kosher authority for kosher certification, the certifying Rabbi seeing that the fellow was not kidding said to him, "Listen, the ingredients may be kosher, but I cannot give a *hechsher* (kosher stamp of approval) which implies not only that it is kosher, but that it's 'proper' to eat." Keeping kosher means more than what's in the ingredients. At the highest level, it also involves a sensitivity that runs deeply in the identity of the Jew.

Over the course of time (it could be weeks or years) one might hope to deepen that sensitivity, each person in accordance with what is possible for him or her to accomplish personally.

When one embarks upon a spiritual journey, it is wise to check in from time to time with a fellow observant Jew whom one respects. This person could be a Rabbi, a teacher, or simply a knowledgeable friend whom one holds in high regard. Having such a *mashpia* (spiritual guide or mentor) can help an individual precisely in an area such as the "imitation non-kosher food" department, where there are shades of gray in the strict *halachic* (Jewish legal) sense. One small step in the right direction might yield powerful positive results; moving in the wrong direction could cause the opposite effect, God forbid.

DAY 6

Definitions of
Common Kosher Terms

*T*here are dozens of special words and terms used in the world of kosher observance, and at this point it is worthwhile to spend some time to become familiar with them. Many are in Hebrew and others are in Yiddish. While you do not have to memorize each one, it is worthwhile to study them all as it will help you build a better understanding of how kosher law works, and also know what these words or terms mean when you come across them later on. Let's get started.

Batel B'Shishim	Hebrew for "nullified in sixty." This term is used when, for example, a tiny amount of dairy falls into a pot of beef or chicken soup. If it is not recognizable, does not add taste or modify the product, and the ratio is 1 part (or less) to 60 parts, then the smaller part is said to be "nullified" and the food remains kosher. Be aware that this is not applicable in all situations, nor with all foods.
Bishul Akum	Hebrew for food completely "cooked by a non-Jew." This food is not kosher.
Bishul Yisrael	Hebrew for food "cooked by a Jew."
B'racha	Hebrew for "blessing," recited before performing certain *mitzvot* (commandments) and before and after consuming food or drink.
B'racha L'Vatala	Hebrew for a "blessing recited in vain." Since it is forbidden to say God's name in vain, one cannot recite a blessing (which contains God's name) for no purpose.
Challah	Hebrew for the "portion of dough" taken from a large batch of dough and burned, to commemorate the portion of dough donated to the priests in the times of the Holy Temple; also refers to traditional Shabbat and holiday braided bread.
Chametz	Hebrew for "leavened." It refers to fermented or leavened wheat, barley, oats, rye, or spelt, that are prohibited on Passover.

Chalav Akum	Hebrew for all dairy products "not supervised by a Jew" from the beginning of the milking until the end of production. Such dairy products are not kosher.
Chalav Stam	Hebrew for dairy products that were not supervised by a Jew from the beginning of the milking, but instead "relies on general governmental oversight" of dairy farms.
Chalav Yisrael	Hebrew for dairy products "supervised by a Jew" from the beginning of the milking until the end of production.
Chumra	Hebrew for "stringency." It refers to going beyond the letter of the law.
Fleishig	Yiddish for "meaty." It refers to all meat and poultry products, including foods prepared with, or on, utensils normally used for meat products. It can also refer to a person's status (i.e., "I am fleishig." Meaning, "I have eaten a meat product and cannot eat any dairy until the required time has lapsed [i.e., six hours]").
Glatt Kosher	Glatt in Yiddish means "smooth." When used in the context of kosher meats, it means that the lungs of a slaughtered animal are free of imperfections that might render the animal non-kosher. Sometimes minor lesions are allowed and, in these cases, the meat is technically kosher. Glatt kosher connotes a "higher standard," meaning meat from an animal with completely

smooth lungs (i.e., kosher with no compromises). Also refers to food establishments that keep a very high kosher standard.

Hagalah	Hebrew for "purging" or "boiling," and refers to the process of kosherizing a utensil by immersing it in boiling water.
Halacha	Hebrew for "path" or "way." Refers to all Biblical and Rabbinic laws that guide the daily life of a Jewish person.
Hashgacha	Hebrew for "supervision." Usually refers to food prepared under the supervision of a God-fearing Jewish kosher expert or certifying agency (i.e., "The food is under x hashgacha").
Hechsher	Hebrew for "certification" or "approval," and often refers to the sign or symbol of a certifying kosher agency.
Heter	Hebrew for "unbinding" or "release." Here it refers to finding permissible ways to deal with a particular kosher dilemma. It can also include alleviating certain stringencies within the kosher dietary laws under exceptional circumstances (but by no means the law itself). Also, a heter is only granted by an expert Rabbi who has reviewed the circumstance in great detail.
Kosher	Hebrew for "fit" or "proper." Dietary laws defining the foods permissible for consumption by a Jew.
Kashering/ Kosherizing	The process of making a utensil or piece of equipment fit for use with kosher food. It also refers to the process of soaking and salting kosher meats before they can be consumed.

Kosher for Passover	Refers to foods that do not contain any leaven, which is forbidden on the eight-day Passover holiday.
Libun	Hebrew for "firing" or "purging." The process of kosherizing a utensil, stovetop, or oven with fire (i.e., using a blowtorch) until the object glows red- or white-hot.
Machmir	Hebrew for being "stringent." Like the term Chumra, this refers to taking upon oneself an extra measure of stringency, to make sure one does not violate any law in the Torah, (e.g., "I am very machmir when it comes to choosing where I eat out.")
Maarat Ayin	Hebrew for "creating an appearance of wrong-doing."
Mashgiach	Hebrew for "supervisor." It refers to the person responsible for ensuring that the food served or sold is kosher. A proper mashgiach is a God-fearing religious Jew, an expert in the kosher dietary laws, and someone thoroughly familiar with the operation he is entrusted to oversee.
Mehadrin	Hebrew for "those who beautify." There are many instances when one can choose to be lenient or more stringent in *mitzvah* (commandment) observance. Mehadrin is about doing a mitzvah in the most perfect and beautiful way possible — without resorting to leniencies or looking for "loopholes."
Mevushal	Hebrew for "cooked" or "boiled." It refers to wine that has been boiled so that it is no longer considered "sacramental

wine" for use in the Holy Temple, thus remaining kosher even if handled by non-Jews.

Mikvah	Hebrew for "body of collected water" or "pool of water set aside for ritual immersion." In the context of kosher, it refers to the body of water used in the process of immersing new utensils (or utensils kosherized for the first time) made of certain materials (i.e., metal or glass) before they are used for food.
Milchig	Yiddish for "dairy." It refers to all dairy products, including foods prepared with or on utensils normally used for dairy products. It can also refer to the status of a person (i.e., "I am milchig." Meaning, "I have eaten a dairy product and cannot eat meat until the required time has lapsed [i.e., one hour]").
Mitzvah/ Mitzvot	Hebrew for "commandment," but implying an opportunity to "connect" to God. There are 613 mitzvot in the Torah, 248 positive commandments ("do"), and 365 negative commandments ("do not").
Pareve	Hebrew for "kosher-neutral." It describes foods that are neither meaty nor dairy, do not contain any meaty or dairy derivatives, and have not been cooked or mixed with any meaty or dairy food. The term also applies to utensils and equipment that have never been used for meaty or dairy foods (i.e., eggs, vegetables, fish, etc.).

Pas (or Pat) Akum	Hebrew for "bread (or other baked goods) baked by a non-Jew" in a non-commercial setting. These are not kosher.
Pas (or Pat) Palter	Hebrew, referring to "bread (or other baked goods) baked by a non-Jewish commercial bakery." Some hold it is permissible in a city where Pas Yisrael is impossible to obtain.
Pas (or Pat) Yisrael	Hebrew, referring to "bread (or other baked goods) baked by a Jew," or a Jew having some involvement that is integral to the baking process (i.e., kindling or adding to the fire in the oven).
Shechita	Hebrew for "slaughtering." It refers to the Biblical method of slaughtering kosher animals.
Sha'alah	Hebrew for "question." It refers to seeking a ruling from a Rabbi who is an expert in kosher law (for example, "I put a meaty spoon in a dairy pot of food on the stove. What should I do with the spoon and the pot, and what is the status of the food?").
Shochet	Hebrew for "expert ritual slaughterer." One who is proficient in the laws and practical aspects of kosher ritual slaughter and has been tested and certified as such by a respected *Halachic* (Jewish legal) rabbinical authority.
Tevilat Keilim	Hebrew for "immersing utensils." It refers to the process of immersing new utensils (or utensils kosherized for the first time) made of certain materials (i.e., metal or glass) in a mikvah before they are used for food.

Torah	Hebrew for "teaching" or "instruction." It includes both the Written and Oral Law of the Bible. It also describes the *Five Books of Moses.*
Toiveling	Yiddish for "immersing utensils." It refers to the process of immersing new (or utensils kosherized for the first time) utensils made of certain materials (i.e., metal or glass) in a mikvah before they are used for food.
T'reif	Hebrew for "torn." It generally refers to any food or item that is not kosher. It is derived from the Torah's commandment forbidding Jews from eating meat "torn" by a predator.
Yayin Nesech	Hebrew for "gentile wine" used for idolatrous purposes, and is considered not kosher.

DAY 7

The Personal Impact
of Going Kosher

For many people, the biggest obstacle to going kosher is concern over how the change will affect them and their family. They may be apprehensive that they will lose friends or upset relationships. Or they may have qualms that once they commit to keeping kosher, it will be too difficult to maintain long-term, making the whole effort a waste of time, energy, and money. The truth is that personal, business, and social obligations can test one's commitment to kosher observance, and you may (and probably will) encounter pressure to compromise. But with the proper modicum of Jewish pride and self-respect, plus lots of tact, not only will you persevere, you will flourish, both physically and spiritually. How can we be so sure of this? The *Talmud* states that God doesn't make unreasonable demands of His creations. If God gives us a commandment, such as keeping Kosher, He surely gives us the ability to fulfill it.

WHAT TO EXPECT WHEN YOU "GO KOSHER."

Varying circumstances will call for different courses of action for different people as they "go kosher." Generally speaking, though, here's your chance to look before you leap.

AT HOME

- You'll have your kitchen kosherized by a knowledgeable friend or kosher expert. He or she can do the kosherizing for you or help you kosherize your dishes, pots, pans, utensils, ovens, stove-tops, sinks, etc. — basically all items that were used to prepare and cook food.

I was so excited to have my kitchen kosherized. I felt I had a fresh start to my life.

AVIVA K., AGE 27
SYDNEY, AU

As mentioned earlier, kosherizing is generally done by dipping the items in a huge pot of boiling water, or by heating them with fire (i.e., with a blowtorch). The technique applied will depend on the item's material and how it was used. Some items (i.e. certain china, glassware, plastics, etc.) cannot be easily kosherized and will need to be replaced. Your kosher expert will help you know what can stay and what must go.

- You'll go through your refrigerator, freezer, pantry, and spice rack and remove all non-kosher items. You can donate them to a non-Jewish thrift shop or give them to a non-Jewish friend (it is forbidden to give them to another Jew).

- You'll designate exclusive areas in your cabinets, drawers, and on your countertops for meaty and dairy utensils and food preparation areas.

- You'll designate which ovens and cooktops you will use for meaty and for dairy cooking.

- Once all your cooking utensils, kitchenware, stoves, and cooktops are kosherized (or even before), you'll purchase any other items that you will need. This could include another set of dishes, assorted pots, pans, and utensils that will serve all your meat and dairy cooking and eating needs. Having different patterns or colors on your dairy and meat utensils will help you to distinguish them. Some people use special heat-resistant stickers for pots and pans (i.e. red for meat, blue or yellow for dairy, and green for pareve). You can find these in many Jewish bookstores.

- Once you have your kosher kitchen properly set up, you're ready to go! Remember not to mix dairy and meat utensils and pots. If they get mixed up (which commonly happens in the beginning), don't panic! Often the food

I invited all of my friends and made a big party on the day we kosherized my kitchen. It was very meaningful for everyone.

SUSAN M., AGE 41
MEMPHIS, TN

becomes non-kosher and the pots or utensils have to be re-kosherized. However, before you do anything, consult a kosher expert. You may find that your problem is not as bad as you think.

SHOPPING

- You'll look for processed and packaged food items that have a reliable kosher symbol on the package. Luckily there are thousands of choices available!

- You'll become familiar with your local kosher stores, which may also include a butcher's shop and bakery.

COOKING

- You'll start building a collection of kosher recipes and cookbooks.

- You'll learn how to prepare your favorite dishes using only kosher ingredients and combinations.

PERSONALLY

- You'll provide spiritual nourishment and fulfillment for your Jewish soul.

- You'll gain peace of mind knowing that you're being true to yourself and to your religion.

- You'll learn self-discipline, which you can carry over to other areas of your life.

- You'll be teaching your children to cherish spiritual values over physical delights.

- You'll be doing your part in Creation, by infusing the *mitzvot* (commandments) and good deeds you do with appropriate and holy energy forces.

- You'll enjoy a multitude of spiritual benefits from keeping kosher, both in this world and the World to Come.

FAMILY

- Keeping kosher as a family draws the family together as you all share a common practice.

- If some members of your family are not yet kosher-observant, they might be upset that you can't eat food prepared in their non-kosher kitchen. This may also include family events where non-kosher catered food is served. This is a challenge, no doubt. But there are several ways to address the issue.

Speak to the most sensitive (and spiritually sensible) person in the family. Sometimes it helps to get another family member to understand and intervene.

Keep in touch with family members so that they don't think that you've deserted them, or begun to look down on them.

You can offer to bring your own food.

You can offer to pay the difference between non-kosher and kosher food, so that everyone will eat kosher.

You can offer to bring everything in and eat on paper plates, using plastic utensils, etc.

My parents thought I went off the deep end, until they saw how fulfilled I was by practicing Judaism unashamedly.

DEVORAH K., AGE 36
LOS ANGELES, CA

I found that keeping kosher connects me with Jews all over the world.

SARAH F., AGE 33
QUEENS, NY

If you come up with a situation that requires extra sensitivity, ask your Rabbi or kosher expert for advice.

SOCIALLY

• You'll have to decide where you will eat out and in whose homes you will eat.

• You'll let your friends know that you are keeping kosher, which limits your options of where to eat out (or what to eat in). You can introduce friends and relatives to the kosher establishments around town.

AT WORK

• You'll kosherize (or replace) your metal, glass, or ceramic cups and utensils.

• You'll pay more attention to the foods you buy and the places you eat, making sure they have either a kosher symbol or are prepared under reliable kosher certification.

• You'll have to plan in advance to ensure that you will have kosher food at business meetings, business lunches and dinners, during travel, etc.

• You'll have lunch at a local kosher restaurant or you'll have it brought in from a kosher caterer, or you'll bring something from home.

AFTER GOING KOSHER PEOPLE REPORT FEELING

- More in control of their lives.

- Healthier.

- More vibrant.

- More spiritual.

- A deep sense of purpose.

- Kinship with other Jews.

- Connected to ancestors in a tangible way.

- At peace with themselves.

- And, never looked back!

Of all the "feel good" Jewish activism I did, nothing satisfied me more than going kosher.

JESSICA A., AGE 26
ORLANDO, FL

TODAY'S ACTION
Consider the inter-
personal effects of
"going kosher."

DAY 8

Preparing Yourself
& Your Family

$\mathcal{F}$or those raised in a kosher observant household, keeping kosher is easy and comes naturally. However, for those growing up any other way, going kosher represents a major change, one that affects nearly every aspect of life. This is especially true when making the change within a family where other family members are not ready (or willing) to go kosher presently. Regardless of the circumstances, the approach that works best is one that is neither antagonistic ("holier than thou") nor

I went out of my way to be extra sensitive to my friends. It's what kept us together.

LEAH K., AGE 39
PHILADELPHIA, PA

tramples on the space and feelings of others (i.e., "my way or no food!"). Additionally, the value of cooperation and education cannot be over-emphasized. There is no point in making your kitchen kosher before you and everyone else living with you know how to keep it kosher, or you will quickly have to kosherize it again.

If you're lucky, your friends who are not kosher-observant will openly respect you and your commitment. They may become inspired and follow your path at some later time (but don't expect or demand it). However, you may also find several who will tease you or even become emotional, claiming that "you've changed." Patiently let them know them that this is a choice about personal growth and about becoming more in touch with your Jewishness, and that it does not diminish your love or respect for them. As for others who react negatively, you'll simply have to learn to ignore their remarks, knowing that, as a Jew, you are doing the right thing.

GOING KOSHER WHEN LIVING ON YOUR OWN (SINGLE, IN COLLEGE, ETC.)

This is probably the easiest time to go kosher, and, if this is you, you should take advantage of the opportunity. Since you are living on your own, you can shop for and prepare your food any way you want. The most complicated issue you will face will be visiting family or friends who don't yet keep kosher. You'll have to explain why you can't eat the food they prepare (i.e., even if the food is "kosher," the utensils, ovens, dinnerware, etc. are not.) You'll have to explain what needs to be done in order for you to eat there (e.g., bringing in food from a kosher deli or restaurant, using plasticware and disposable plates, heating the food in a kosher-compliant manner, etc.). In any case, remind yourself and those around you that in a home that is not kosher observant, it's the food that's non-kosher, not the people!

Getting started:

- Study everything you can about kosher.

- Spend time in a kosher kitchen, either by visiting a friend's house or by inviting yourself over to your local Orthodox Rabbi's home on a Friday afternoon to observe Shabbat food preparations. You'll learn a lot from seeing a kosher kitchen in action.

- Enlist the help of a local kosher expert or Orthodox Rabbi.

- Write out your reasons for going kosher. This will help you explain it to others.

- Proceed to the next chapter ("Day 9").

GOING KOSHER AS A FAMILY (LIVING WITH PARENTS, MARRIED, ETC.)

Going kosher in a family can be pretty straightforward and pleasant. Most of the time, it brings the family closer together; since everyone is in agreement, the process is relatively easy. Going kosher as a family also means that you'll be able to encourage and support each other.

When my family and friends saw that I was determined, they respected my choice.

HEATHER W., AGE 22
NEW YORK, NY

What worked in our own marriage was respecting each other's path and pace.

JEFF A., AGE 47
CLIFTON, NJ

Getting started:

• Study everything you can about kosher.

• Enlist the help of a local kosher expert or Orthodox Rabbi.

• Educate family members. Study books on kosher together and discuss what you've learned.

• Have a meeting to set out "the plan" and to make sure everyone is on board.

• Remind everyone of the beauty of doing *mitzvot* (commandments), and how this mitzvah in particular is important for the family's Jewish identity.

• Give each member of the family a specific topic to study, or delegate part of the process (cleaning, spotting kosher symbols while shopping, etc.). Find ways to involve everyone.

• When dealing with adolescent children, or other family members who are not fully "on board," remember that going kosher is a big change for everyone. Consider their feelings. If they resist, come to some mutual understanding that works for everyone in the short term. Once you've passed that hurdle, you can work towards the long term. A competent kosher expert or Orthodox Rabbi can help you come up with workable solutions for most situations.

• Proceed to the next chapter ("Day 9").

GOING KOSHER ALONE WITHIN A FAMILY (LIVING AT HOME WITH PARENTS, MARRIED, ETC.)

This is definitely more challenging, but still doable.

Common Challenges Include:

- Keeping your food and utensils separate.

- Keeping good relations all around (this is your responsibility!).

- Dealing with pressure to eat out with family at places that are not kosher.

Getting Started:

- Study everything you can about kosher.

- Enlist the help of a local kosher expert or Orthodox Rabbi.

- Have an informal chat with your close family members and friends to let them know about your decision to go kosher, and to reassure them that you still love and respect them. Make certain that they understand that this change is about adding holiness to your life. Don't preach or try to "convert" your family or friends who may not yet be keeping kosher. For now, focus on your own personal objective of going kosher. And remember, the only effective way to lead is by being a pleasant example.

- Proceed to the next chapter ("Day 9").

Sometimes I felt so alone in my kosher observance, but then I realized I am connected to my ancestors and to Jews around the world.

KATHY S., AGE 29
MIAMI, FL

TODAY'S ACTION
Time to make a
practical plan of
action.

DAY 9

Making a
Practical Plan

*M*aking the transition to kosher a pleasant and trouble-free experience requires thought and planning. If there is one thing you'll get to love about kosher, it's that it is all about being thorough. The kosherizing of your kitchen is probably the most complex step in going kosher, and should only be done once you've worked out the usage details that works for your own kitchen. Before you call to engage a Rabbi or kosher expert to do the kosehrization, you will need to plan how you want to divide your kitchen for meat and dairy use. This chapter will allow you to make sense of the process, helping you get organized and prepared.

PLANNING

- Make a complete inventory of your kitchen so that it will be easy to visualize exactly what you have. List everything, including pots and pans, silverware, cups, plates, appliances — all items that come into contact with food. This will help you plan what items you'll set aside for meat, for dairy, and for pareve use.

Going kosher helped me become more organized, generally.

MALKA K., AGE 36
ORLANDO, FL

- Plan your kosher kitchen (it is a good idea to enlist the help of a local kosher expert or Orthodox Rabbi to help guide you through this stage). With a pad of paper in hand, visualize how you will use different areas of your kitchen, including the counter space, utensils, appliances, etc. Sketch a diagram of your kitchen and indicate what part of your counter will be for dairy, and what part will be for meat.

- Determine which items can be kosherized and which will be discarded (i.e., given to a thrift store or non-Jewish friend) and replaced with new ones (see "Days 11-13").

- Spend time in a kosher kitchen of a friend, Rabbi, or relative. Watch and/or help cook a meal. Learn the practicalities of kosher cooking.

- Visit your food market to familiarize yourself with food products that have kosher certification (see "Day 17").

- List pantry items that you use regularly that are not kosher and look for kosher substitutes in your favorite food store.

- Choose several "going kosher" practice steps and begin observing them beforehand, such as not eating obviously non-kosher foods (i.e., ham, shellfish, etc.), not cooking meat and dairy together, waiting between eating meat and dairy, and so on.

- Locate a mikvah for immersing utensils prior to their first use (see "Day 14").

- Designate a cabinet or storage space for Passover items (see "Day 26").

- Make a list of your questions as you go through this book (and others) to discuss with your local Orthodox Rabbi and kosher expert.

- Purchase kosher cookbooks, including one for Passover cooking.

- Pick a realistic target date for your "kosherizing day."

- If your kitchen door post does not have a kosher mezuzah (small parchment scrolls inscribed with portions of Torah, rolled in a case and hung on door posts in Jewish homes), now is an opportune time to purchase one from a reliable source (i.e., Judaica stores that specialize in religious goods). Better even, get mezuzot for all the doors of your house. (Bathrooms and small closets/ areas less than 36 sq. ft. are exempt). Having mezuzot in one's home add holiness and brings great blessings.

The mezuzah case is nailed (or glued) to the right door post at a slight angle (pointing towards the room entering), slightly above the average shoulder height.

Before affixing the mezuzah, the following blessing is recited:

בָּרוּךְ אַתָּה יְיָ, אֱלֹהֵינוּ מֶלֶךְ הָעוֹלָם, אֲשֶׁר קִדְּשָׁנוּ בְּמִצְוֹתָיו,
וְצִוָּנוּ, לִקְבּוֹעַ מְזוּזָה:

Böruch atöh adonöy, elohaynu melech hö-olöm, asher kid'shönu b'mitzvosöv, v'tzivönu, lik-bo-a m'zuzöh.

Blessed are You, Lord our God, King of the universe, Who has sanctified us with His command-ments, and commanded us to affix a mezuzah.

It is customary to touch or kiss the Mezuzah when entering or leaving a room.

It is important to have the mezuzot of your home inspected by a compe-tent, God-fearing scribe every few years to ensure that they are valid (ink on the parchment tends to fade or crack with age rendering the mezuzah unfit, requiring it to be replaced with a new one).

TODAY'S ACTION
Take some first steps in observing the kosher dietary laws.

DAY 10

First Steps in Going Kosher

*T*here are two basic ways people approach voluntary changes in lifestyle — jumping right in, or taking little steps. When it comes to kosher, no one denies that it is vital to stop eating non-kosher foods right away and to go completely kosher immediately. Indeed, some people have successfully gone kosher cold-turkey. Nevertheless, most of those who succeeded did so in slow but steady steps. Of course, your goal is to go kosher quickly, successfully, and permanently. However,

101

I remember being very excited when I started keeping kosher out of the house. It was like my secret Jewish space no one could intrude upon.

NATALIE C., AGE 25, S. DIEGO, CA

doing too much too soon can cause you to become overwhelmed and maybe a bit discouraged, putting yourself at the risk of going right back to the starting point. Our advice is that once you resolve to go kosher, go ahead with determination, yet respect your limits, recognize your strengths and weaknesses, and set for yourself a realistic path.

In all cases, a healthy sense of urgency is always good, for kosher observance isn't an "optional" mitzvah. (They're called commandments — not options!) Therefore, the sooner you become completely kosher, the better it will be for your body and soul.

Finally, know that progressing through kosher observance to a certain point and not continuing further (i.e., "I eat kosher at home, but not outside") is not keeping kosher as it is meant to be in the Torah. Essentially, resolving to make only a partial commitment for the rest of your life would mean that you are keeping kosher on your own terms, not God's, which essentially means it is more about you than about a relationship with Him. Just as there is no "almost" Jewish or "sometimes" Jewish, one should ultimately progress from "almost" kosher, or "sometimes" kosher, to "always" kosher.

SOME FIRST-STEPS

- Finish reading this book (without skipping chapters!).
- Stop eating obviously non-kosher items (ham, shellfish, etc.).
- Spend time in a kosher kitchen, watching, helping, and learning.

- Visit your local food market and look for foods with a kosher symbol on the packaging. Familiarize yourself with the different symbols (see "Day 17").

- Practice waiting the required waiting period between eating meaty and dairy foods, and dairy and meaty foods (see "Day 5").

- Substitute non-kosher foods in your pantry with ones that have a kosher symbol on the package.

- Separate meat and dairy foods and utensils.

- Modify your favorite recipes using only kosher ingredients and combinations.

- Stop eating at non-kosher restaurants.

- Stop buying all non-kosher foods. Buy only foods with a kosher symbol on the package (even if you haven't kosherized your kitchen yet).

- Talk with someone who keeps kosher.

TODAY'S ACTION
Plan the kosherizing
of your kitchen.

DAY 11

Transforming
the Kitchen

*A*s the heart and hearth of your home, the kitchen is the source of both physical and spiritual nourishment. In order for a non-kosher kitchen to become kosher, it must undergo a through cleaning followed by expert kosherizing. This cleaning also includes eliminating all non-kosher food items and vessels or utensils that cannot be made kosher. The actual kosherizing process requires dipping certain items in boiling water and subjecting others to intense heat with fire, followed by the immersion of utensils in a valid *mikvah* (pool of water set aside for ritual immersion) or natural body of water (i.e., ocean or lake). The kosherizing process also includes training and educating everyone living in the home on how to maintain the kitchen's kosher status once it is properly kosherized.

Kosherizing your kitchen for the first time should be done by a Jewish person who has the proper experience, expertise, and equipment. Your local Orthodox Rabbi can help you find such an expert (if he doesn't do it himself).

WHAT IS A "KOSHER KITCHEN"?

By this time, you've already inventoried your kitchen and decided which items will stay and which will go, and you've figured out how you will use the counter and cabinet space. Now it's time for the details.

A kosher kitchen is one in which only kosher food is prepared and eaten (even food that is not for your consumption, [i.e., a worker's lunch]). Non-kosher food is never allowed into the kitchen since it can become mixed with kosher food and jeopardize the kosher status of the entire kitchen.

An efficient kosher kitchen is arranged so that meat or dairy foods and utensils never mix, for if they do, they (and any food involved) often become non-kosher and need to be re-kosherized.

Separate pots, pans, serving utensils, dishware, cutlery, etc., are used for meat or dairy and are stored in separate drawers and cabinets. Having distinct patterns or colors for dishes, serving plates, and the like (i.e. red for meat, blue for dairy, and green for pareve), and different designs on cutlery, make it easy to tell them apart.

Many kosher kitchens will have two stovetops, two ovens, and two sinks — one used exclusively for meat and the other for dairy. This is the best option. Often, however, financial and practical issues (such as renting as opposed to owning your home) do not permit such luxury. In such a case, the single oven is kosherized and allocated for either meat or dairy, and a separate dedicated toaster oven or convection oven is used for the other. Burners on the stovetop can also be kosherized and allocated for exclusive use for meat or dairy cooking.

A kosher expert can help you maximize your kitchen, counter, cabinet, and cooktop space for convenience and productivity. In addition, he or she can offer practical insight and tips based on years of hands-on experience.

Overall, making a kosher kitchen is easier today than ever before, as kitchen appliances and kitchenware are becoming more affordable for everyone.

WHAT DOES "KOSHERIZING" DO?

Kosherizing restores most items, appliances, and surfaces to their original neutral state, permitting them to be used with kosher food. Once the item has been properly kosherized, you are able to designate it for either meat or milk use.

WHO CAN KOSHERIZE MY KITCHEN?

Even for those familiar with all the laws of kosher, kosherizing an entire kitchen is a complex task that needs to be done with great care and precision. While there is no reason you couldn't kosherize your kitchen yourself, it is highly advisable to get

I was so nervous leading up to the kosherizing day, but I prepared well, so it really went smoothly.

CHANA J., AGE 28
LOS ANGELES, CA

an expert to do the initial kosherizing. Today, you can find an Orthodox Rabbi who is a kosher expert in almost every city in America. Call around, ask your friends, or do a quick online search.

Don't worry about the cost of hiring a kosher expert. Assuming they have the time, most experts won't charge you anything to answer your questions. They may not charge anything (or very little) to kosherize your kitchen either, because it is a tremendous *mitzvah* (commandment) to help a Jewish family to go kosher. It is, however, appropriate to offer something when the job is done, in appreciation for their time, effort, and hard work.

BEFORE THE BIG DAY

- Buy a supply of paper plates, plastic cutlery, and cups. These will come in handy during the transition period.

- Go through your kitchen (refrigerator, freezer, pantry, spice rack, etc.) and gather all foods that do not bear a kosher symbol or were prepared or used in the non-kosher kitchen. This includes open jars and even open packages of kosher food as non-kosher utensils may have already rendered them non-kosher.

- Thoroughly scrub and clean all items to be kosherized, including the surfaces of stoves, ovens, and countertops, making sure to remove all food particles and stains. It is impossible to kosherize an item or surface that has dirt, grime, or rust residue (which is why it is close to impossible to properly kosherize dishwashers — it is nearly impossible to completely remove all food particles).

- All items to be kosherized must not be used for at least 24 hours prior to kosherizing them. If you do use them, you will have to postpone their kosherizing for another 24 hours.

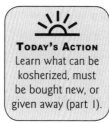

TODAY'S ACTION
Learn what can be
kosherized, must
be bought new, or
given away (part 1).

DAY 12

Countertops, Appliances,
Sinks, Stoves & Ovens

*A*s mentioned above, one of the most basic and fundamental concepts of kosher is the separation of meat and milk. Therefore, a successful kosher kitchen is arranged so that this separation is preserved throughout the process of food preparation, serving, eating, and cleaning. Any cross-mixing between meat and dairy, which can easily happen in a busy kitchen, can render the food and utensils involved as non-kosher, and the utensils must be pulled from service until it is clarified whether or not they have to be kosherized (usually verified by asking an Orthodox Rabbi or kosher expert). Therefore, careful planning at the pre-kosherizing stage is the key to maintaining a smoothly running kosher kitchen for years to come.

SURFACES & MATERIALS

Materials play a big role in kosherizing a kitchen. Whether manufactured from metal, glass, or ceramic, each kind of material absorbs and purges flavors differently, and is treated differently when it comes to kosherizing them.

COUNTERTOPS, CABINETS, DRAWERS

Depending on the material they are made of, most countertops need to be kosherized before using them for kosher food. Consult your local kosher expert to determine what kosherizing treatment your particular countertops require. If they are made of a material that cannot be kosherized, he will advise what other remedies are available to you. Cabinets and drawers generally need only be cleaned really well before use with kosher food or utensils.

Designate exclusive areas for your meat and dairy utensils and countertops for food preparation. If an area will be used for meat and dairy (separately), separate trivets, cutting boards, and coverings should be used.

It is a good idea to label cabinets and cookware "DAIRY," "MEAT," or "PAREVE" to help remember which is which and what goes where.

REFRIGERATORS & FREEZERS

Refrigerators and freezers may be used to store both meat and dairy foods. Just make sure to cover or wrap the food well so that it won't leak or drip onto nearby items. Also, never put hot meaty or dairy foods in the fridge or freezer, since heat transfers flavor and can affect the kosher status of nearby items (including the shelf itself). Therefore, always allow things to cool down before putting them in. It is also wise to use a trivet when possible.

Refrigerators are kosherized by thoroughly scrubbing them clean and purging any glass shelves with boiling water.

DISHWASHERS

A dishwasher should only be used exclusively for meat or for dairy. This is because it is very difficult to kosherize a dishwasher as the racks and interior shell are made from plastics and rubbers that cannot survive the heat of the kosherizing process. To remedy this, you may purchase new racks and replace the shell. Nevertheless, most used dishwashers contain food particles buried so deep inside the unit, it's almost impossible to get them out. If possible, it is best to replace the entire dishwasher.

TOASTER OVENS & SANDWICH MAKERS

Toasters, including toaster ovens, cannot be easily kosherized and are better replaced. Sandwich- and waffle-makers, including burger-makers, may be kosherized if all the surfaces are metal and can be completely removed and scrubbed clean, then purged with a blow torch until they glow red- or white-hot. Otherwise, they should be replaced. Many *Halachic* (Jewish legal) authorities advise not to kosherize non-stick metal kitchen appliances, as they are impossible to completely purge them with fire.

MICROWAVE OVENS

It is best to designate a microwave oven for either meat or dairy use; it should not be used for both. Many purchase a second microwave for use with the opposite category of food as the first. Microwave ovens can be kosherized by thoroughly cleaning them, placing a cup of water inside, and "nuking it" until the water is heavily steaming (about ten minutes, depending on the wattage of your microwave).

OTHER SMALL APPLIANCES

Small appliances such as blenders, mixers, grinders, etc., may be used for both meat and dairy if one has separate attachments and bowls for meat and dairy use. The entire base must be thoroughly cleaned between uses.

THE KITCHEN SINK

Ideally, you should have a sink for meat and a sink for dairy use, since this helps to keep everything separate. However, many people do not have the luxury of installing a second sink (but do keep it in mind when you plan your next kitchen!).

Sinks that are made from stainless steel or other metals may be kosherized with boiling water. Sinks made from Corian and other glass-based materials (including ceramics) cannot be kosherized, but can still be used with certain precautions.

Regardless of the material it is made of, a single sink inevitably becomes non-kosher because it absorbs from both the meaty and dairy utensils being washed in it. Therefore, you should never let anything soak directly in the sink or lay a hot pot inside it. Instead, use different colored sink racks or basins (i.e., red for meaty, or blue for dairy) when needed. Separate sponges, scouring pads, and dish-washing gloves are necessary as well. It is a good idea to also have separate basins for soaking milk and meat items.

If your kitchen has a sink with two wells, or two adjoining sinks, you can designate one for meaty use and the other for dairy. However, be very careful not to allow any hot water or food particles to splash from one side to the other (i.e., when cleaning a chicken or emptying a pot). Many people cover one side when working on the other side. Also consider that in either a single- or double-well sink configuration, the spout on the faucet is to be considered non-kosher and should not come in direct contact with any food or utensils.

Metal sinks are kosherized by thoroughly scrubbing them, allowing them to sit without use for 24 hours, then pouring boiling water over all exposed surfaces.

STOVETOPS

It's best to have separate stovetops for meat and dairy use. However, if you only have one stovetop, you can designate individual burners for meaty and dairy use (for instance, the two on the left are for meat, and the two on the right are for dairy). Needless to say, you should never use the designated meaty burner to cook dairy

We ended up designating our oven as "meaty," and got a small toaster oven for dairy foods.

CLAIRE P., AGE 42
MIAMI, FL

foods, or *vice versa* (without properly kosherizing it in between). You could also simply designate the stovetop as totally meaty, and use separate, freestanding burners for dairy foods.

When using a single stovetop for both meat and dairy, you should never have meaty and dairy pots on top at the same time. Even keeping an empty meaty or dairy pot on the stove while cooking the opposite type of food can introduce kosher problems due to splattering, hot steam, and vapors. In any event, be sure to keep the middle section of the stovetop clean and not allow hot foods to rest directly on it, because at times there will be meaty or dairy spillages, making that area non-kosher.

A vent hood over a stovetop that is used for both meat and dairy could pose a kosher problem. At some point, it becomes saturated with steam and particles of food, which later condense and drip down onto the stovetop's surface, pots, and possibly your food while the stovetop is in active use. Therefore, you should make sure to clean it regularly.

SEAMLESS GLASS STOVETOPS

Seamless glass stovetops are problematic for kosher purposes. Since they are made of one continuous surface and not separate burners, you can't split them into separate meaty and dairy sections. In addition, any meaty or dairy spills flow across the entire surface, making the other side non-kosher. This means that if you already have a glass stovetop, you should devote it exclusively for meat or dairy use. If you are purchasing a new stovetop, it is better not to get a sealed glass cooktop in the first place, since it is difficult (if not impossible) to properly kosherize it should a kosher problem present itself in the future.

OVENS

A single oven should be designated exclusively for meaty or dairy use. If your particular oven vents vapors from the oven up to the stovetop, then the burners nearest to the vent should be designated the same status as the oven. For practical purposes, many designate their oven as meaty, and purchase a separate electric toaster oven for dairy use.

If you have a double oven, meaning one oven is on top of the other, you may want to designate one for meaty and one for dairy use. Make sure, however, that the ovens are truly independent, and that no steam goes from one into the other. If this is not the case, they cannot be divided and both must be designated as either meaty or dairy exclusively.

Kosherizing a stovetop and oven involves the following steps:

First, the stovetop and oven are scrubbed spotlessly clean, removing all food residue and rust. This cleaning is very important as they cannot be kosherized if there are any food particles, fats, rust, or other residues remaining.

Second, after the cleaning, the stovetop and oven are not used for 24 hours prior to kosherizing them.

Third, after 24 hours have passed, the grates and interior of the oven are heated with a blow torch until they glow red- or white-hot. Alternatively, some authorities permit setting the oven to it's highest temperature for at least an hour (instead of using a blow torch). Consult your kosher expert.

An oven that has a self-cleaning feature may be kosherized by running the highest setting self-cleaning cycle for at least 4 hours (it generally takes this much time for it to reach the highest temperature). You may also put the grates from the stovetop into the oven for the cleaning cycle to kosherize them at the same time.

When kosherizing an oven using the self-cleaning cycle, remember to first clean the oven and racks extremely well, removing all food residue and rust, for otherwise the kosherizing is ineffective and invalid.

Many Halachic authorities hold that when running a full, self-cleaning cycle, the oven does not have to stand idle for 24 hours. All agree, however, that if possible, it is preferable to let it sit without use for 24 hours prior to kosherizing it.

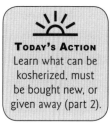

TODAY'S ACTION
Learn what can be kosherized, must be bought new, or given away (part 2).

DAY 13

Pots, Pans, Dishware, Glassware, Cutlery, Etc.

All utensils that were used in a non-kosher kitchen must be thoroughly cleaned, kosherized, and immersed in a *mikvah* (pool of water set aside for ritual immersion, or natural stream, ocean, or lake), before they can be used with kosher food. This includes cutlery, serving utensils, pots, pans, and so on. As mentioned earlier, once everything is properly kosherized, you can designate items for either exclusive meaty or dairy use. To avoid confusion, most people designate their present kitchenware for either meaty or dairy use, and purchase a new set for the other category. This new set may include pots and pans, silverware, knives, cutting boards, serving platters and utensils, salt and pepper shakers, baking pans, sponges, racks and drainers, dish towels, tablecloths, and placemats.

Some will also purchase a third, smaller set of kitchenware for off in the category of "pareve," which is food that is neither meat nor dairy (i.e., eggs, fish, fruits and vegetables, etc.). All non-meat and non-dairy food prepared (exclusively) on these pareve utensils may be served and eaten with meaty or dairy foods (see "Day 22").

MATERIALS IMPACT KOSHER

As mentioned earlier, whether manufactured from metal, glass, or ceramic, each kind of material absorbs and purges fats and flavors differently, and is treated differently when it comes to kosherizing them.

POTS & PANS

Stainless steel, copper, or other metal pots and pans are generally kosherized in boiling water or with a blow torch until they glow red- or white-hot, depending on how they were used. They must first be perfectly clean, including in all crevices (i.e., pot handle joints, etc.) and stand idle for 24 hours.

Non-stick, or enamel-lined baking or frying pans, cannot be kosherized. Certain ceramics pots and pans also cannot be kosherized because they do not purge easily or will break in the boiling water. Consult your kosher expert about any unusual items you might have.

DISHWARE

Dishes that can be kosherized must first be thoroughly cleaned, allowed to stand idle for at least 24 hours, and completely immersed in boiling water. Dishes made from ceramic or porcelain — including fragile chinaware and cups — cannot be kosherized. These items shatter easily at high temperatures, so there is no way to completely purge the non-kosher flavor from them. Consult your kosher expert for guidance if you have such items.

If a beloved set of dishes or china cannot be kosherized, it can indeed be difficult to part with it, but keep in mind that the physical loss is far outweighed by the spiritual gain. Try to view it as a small (or even great) sacrifice for a very important *mitzvah* (commandment) that will pay spiritual dividends for you and your family for years to come.

It was difficult parting with my favorite china, but I've gained so much more from going kosher.

SARAH W., AGE 48, TWIN CITIES, MN

GLASSWARE

According to some authorities, glassware, including Pyrex and Bakelite, cannot be properly kosherized. Therefore, it is best to replace them. According to other authorities, glassware that can withstand boiling water may be kosherized. Alternatively, if the item can withstand the heat of a self-cleaning oven, it may be kosherized by thoroughly cleaning it and then putting it in the oven, running it on the highest-setting self-cleaning cycle. It is best to consult your kosher expert for complete guidance.

CUTLERY & UTENSILS

All cutlery and utensils made from metal, stainless steel, copper, and silver, are easily kosherized. They first must be perfectly clean, including in all crevices (i.e., between the tines of forks, edges of some cups, etc.), stand idle for at least 24 hours, and be immersed in boiling water. Knives and other utensils that have wooden or other handles are difficult to properly clean and cannot be kosherized. This also applies to handles on certain pots. Consult your kosher expert for complete guidance.

RACKS, DISH-DRAINS, TOWELS, SPONGES

Most other non-metal or glass kitchenware may be used after thoroughly scrubbing and cleaning them. But if possible, it is best to get new ones and designate them for exclusive meaty or dairy use.

All sponges, scrubbing brushes, cutting boards, and drying racks should be replaced. Consult your kosher expert for complete guidance.

TODAY'S ACTION
Learn about and perform the immersion of your utensils in a mikvah.

DAY 14

Immersion of Utensils
in a Mikvah

When the Holy Temple stood in Jerusalem, the High Priest would immerse himself in a *mikvah* on Yom Kippur, a ritual pool connected to a reservoir of natural rain-water, before starting his holy duties. This immersion had more to do with spiritual transformation than physical cleanliness. Today, the mikvah still features prominently in Jewish life. It is used privately by married women as an integral part of the laws of family purity, for Jewish conversions, and by men daily or weekly to add an enhanced spiritual dimension to their service to God. The mikvah is also used for immersing new vessels and utensils (including those newly kosherized for the first time), sanctifying and elevating them, making them fit for use with kosher food.

Keeping a kosher home made me rethink my role as a parent from being simply a provider to being an educator.

DEBBIE G., AGE 42,
CLOVER CITY, CA

FROM THE TORAH

When the Jewish people wanted to bring vessels from non-Jewish tribes into their homes, the Torah commanded them to first kosherize the metal utensils using fire. In addition, *"…the gold, the silver, the copper, the iron, the tin, and the lead…you shall pass through water"* (Numbers 31:22-23). Our Sages taught that this is referring to the waters of a mikvah. Nowadays, most new vessels and utensils (see details below) require immersion, regardless of their origins.

YOUR HOME AS A "MINIATURE TEMPLE"

The *Talmud* adds that the Jewish home corresponds to the Holy Temple, the dining table to the altar, and the food that is served to the sacrifices — i.e., they serve as vehicles to draw Godliness and spirituality into the world. Since everything associated with the Holy Temple had to be *"kadosh,"* holy (i.e., elevated above the mundane), it makes sense for this standard to apply to the home. Just as the Holy Temple served as the spiritual hub of the Jewish people, so does the Jewish home. Just as all the vessels and utensils of the Holy Temple were sanctified with additional measures of holiness, so too, do we sanctify the vessels and utensils in our homes.

PRACTICALLY SPEAKING

In practice, before using many kinds of newly purchased (including newly kosherized) vessels and utensils for food preparation, consumption, and storage (i.e., pots, pans, knives, forks, spoons, plates, china, etc.), they have to be immersed in a mikvah or natural body of water (i.e., an ocean or lake). This immersion is required only once during the lifetime of the item, and is performed at any time prior to their first use. Any Jew (over the age of Bar or Bat Mitzvah) can to perform this immersion.

A special blessing is recited before performing the immersion (see below). For the immersion to be valid, the waters of the mikvah or natural body of water must touch all areas of the item. Therefore, items must be carefully cleaned, having all stickers and any remaining sticky residue removed before immersion. In cases where the sticker is part of the item's beauty and value (i.e., the insignia on "Lenox" crystal), the sticker is considered as part of the vessel and may remain on during the immersion.

If, by mistake, a kosher vessel was used before it was immersed in a mikvah, the food may still be eaten (using another utensil), and the non-immersed vessel is set aside and not used until it is properly immersed.

Items kosherized for the first time are immersed only after they are kosherized. If for whatever reason they were immersed before, they should be immersed again.

FINDING A MIKVAH

Nowadays, it is easy to find a mikvah fit according to Jewish law in many cities around the world. A call to the local Orthodox synagogue, or a quick search online will surely turn up several choices. If you cannot find a local mikvah, consult an Orthodox Rabbi about using a nearby natural lake or stream.

WHICH ITEMS REQUIRE IMMERSION?

Vessels and utensils made from metal, silver, copper, gold, and tin require immersion. Most dishware and crockery also require immersion. Since many products are made today from composite or synthetic materials, it is unclear whether these items Biblically require immersion or not. To be sure, they are immersed anyway but without reciting the special blessing (to avoid reciting God's name in vain if the immersion was indeed not Biblically necessary).

ITEMS REQUIRING IMMERSION *WITH* RECITING THE BLESSING

- Metal, steel, silver, copper, and tin pots and pans.

- Silverware.

- Glass or glass derivatives (i.e., Pyrex, Corelle).

- Glazed earthenware, porcelain, and china.

- Water heaters and kettles.

- The removable metal or glass parts of mixers, blenders, and other kitchen equipment that are in contact with food.

ITEMS THAT SHOULD BE IMMERSED *WITHOUT* RECITING THE BLESSING

- Composite items made of two or more materials (i.e., glass or metal utensils with a wooden handle, pans with a non-stick coating, etc.).

- Certain non-disposable plastic items.

ITEMS THAT DO NOT REQUIRE IMMERSION

- Items made of wood.

- Items made of stone.

- Items made of paper.

- Items made of bone.

- Items made of rubber.

- Unglazed Earthenware.

- Corkscrews; all can and bottle openers.

- Disposable utensils not meant for long-term use (plastic-ware, foam cups and plates, aluminum pans, etc.).

- All vessels that are manufactured exclusively by a Jew.

Performing the Immersion

1) Carefully clean each item, removing all packaging and stickers, including any sticky residue. For tough stickers, use an adhesive-dissolving solution.

2) If you have many items, you may immerse several at a time by putting them in a basket or cotton net. In any case, take the first item to be immersed in your right hand and recite the following blessing:

BLESSING WHEN IMMERSING A SINGLE ITEM

בָּרוּךְ אַתָּה יְיָ, אֱלֹהֵינוּ מֶלֶךְ הָעוֹלָם, אֲשֶׁר קִדְּשָׁנוּ בְּמִצְוֹתָיו,
וְצִוָּנוּ, עַל טְבִילַת כֶּלִי:

Böruch atöh adonöy, elohaynu melech hö-olöm, asher kid'shönu b'mitzvosöv,
v'tzivönu, al t'vilas keli.

*Blessed are You, Lord our God, King of the universe, Who has sanctified us with His commandments,
and commanded us concerning the immersion of a vessel.*

BLESSING WHEN IMMERSING MULTIPLE ITEMS

(While reciting the blessing, have in mind all items you will be immersing)

בָּרוּךְ אַתָּה יְיָ, אֱלֹהֵינוּ מֶלֶךְ הָעוֹלָם, אֲשֶׁר קִדְּשָׁנוּ בְּמִצְוֹתָיו,
וְצִוָּנוּ, עַל טְבִילַת כֵּלִים:

Böruch atöh adonöy, elohaynu melech hö-olöm, asher kid'shönu b'mitzvosöv,
v'tzivönu al t'vilas keilim.

*Blessed are You, Lord our God, King of the universe, Who has sanctified us with His commandments,
and commanded us concerning the immersion of vessels.*

3) Immerse the vessel, making sure that it is completely submerged. Loosen your grasp for a second so that water comes all around the item. Bottles and deep pots must be allowed to fill with water in order for the immersion to be valid.

4) Remove the item from the water. Many have the custom to submerge items two additional times, for a total of three plunges.

If you are immersing multiple items, continue immersing the rest, item by item (without reciting a separate blessing).

Following the immersion it is permitted to rinse or wash utensils with soap and cool water in a kosher sink.

TODAY'S ACTION
Begin reciting
blessings before
and after eating
or drinking kosher
food.

DAY 15

Reciting Blessings
Before & After Eating

*I*f you've read the chapters of this book in order, by now you know that kosher food has a powerful spiritual component. To draw out and elevate these elements, Jewish people recite special blessings before and after eating or drinking kosher food. This beautiful *mitzvah* (commandment) reminds us that food consumption is far more than a mere physical process. By reciting the appropriate blessing, we remember the Creator, and become aware that our nourishment is a gift, not an entitlement. Additionally, we are reminded that we are not merely machines processing food into raw energy, but we have the capability, and therefore the responsibility, to elevate this energy to serve a higher purpose.

The unique and timeless blessings also enable us to thank God for the food we eat, much like we were taught to say "please" and "thank you."

WHAT'S A BLESSING?

> *"You shall bless the Lord your God for the good land which He has given you." (Deuteronomy 8:10)*

There are many, many blessings enumerated in Jewish law for different purposes and occasions. The majority of these are recited before performing certain activities and mitzvot; i.e., before and after partaking of kosher food or drink; before lighting candles for Shabbat, etc. The words of the blessings are composed in Hebrew and were formulated by our Sages. Blessings are recited aloud and with complete concentration. Those hearing the recitation of a blessing customarily respond with *"Amein"* (amen, meaning "it is true," or "we are in agreement"). While it is preferable to recite blessings in Hebrew, you can recite them in any language that you understand.

"GOT GRATITUDE"

Blessings not only express thanks to God for our nourishment and delight, but also articulate much deeper sentiments. God could have created the world so that we obtain our sustenance from tasteless matter, such as sand. In His kindness, He created food with myriads of colors, textures, and tastes, and gave us the ability to see, feel, taste, and take pleasure in them. Blessings not only acknowledge this idea, but also remind us to stop and be grateful for our ability to see, feel, taste, and enjoy the food we are about to eat.

GETTING DEEPER

Jewish mystical teachings of *Kabbala* and *Chassidut* enlighten us with profound meanings hidden in the seemingly plain text of these blessings. These teachings show how the blessings that we make serve as conduits and activators to reveal Godliness in this world.

Let us see for ourselves how the words of many blessings that are recited before performing certain mitzvot tell this story:

> "BLESSED ARE YOU, LORD OUR GOD, KING OF THE UNIVERSE, WHO HAS SANCTIFIED US WITH HIS COMMANDMENTS, AND COMMANDED US CONCERNING... [THE MITZVAH IS MENTIONED]"

> *My youngest, who is three, makes all the blessings in Hebrew. It is so beautiful.*
>
> MIRIAM E., AGE 34
> LONG ISLAND, NY

"BLESSED" – The Hebrew word for "blessed" is *Baruch*, which also has the root letters of the Hebrew word *breicha*, a gathering body or pool of water that had been drawn. It also has the letters of *berech*, which means "knee." The knees allow a person to bend. As we bend, we lower our body, as if drawing down from above. Here, both of these meanings reflect our ability to draw Godliness into the world. We are saying in essence, "Allow us, God, to draw Your Godliness into this world with this blessing."

"ARE YOU" – Notice the use of the direct verb "You," addressing God informally, not through His formal Names which describe His Attributes. We are neither referring to Him through an intermediary, but directly. This is an awesome point to reflect upon, and the more we consider it, the more awesome it becomes.

"LORD, OUR GOD" – In Hebrew, the word used for "Lord" represents the transcendent infinity of God as it hovers "above and beyond" this world. The words "our God" refer to the revelation and expression of God as it relates to the world. Here we are asking God to draw new light from the higher realms into the lower ones.

"KING OF THE UNIVERSE" – The Hebrew word for king is "Melech," which in our context means revealed, as a king can only be king when he is revealed to his subjects. The Hebrew word for universe is "olam," which shares the same root as the word helem, meaning hidden. Since Godliness is not completely revealed in creation, one must search for it. Here we are asking God to reveal Himself where and when He seems hidden, both globally and personally in our daily life. We are asking Him, in essence, to become King of the universe — that the entire order of creation should be able to openly see and acknowledge His greatness.

"WHO HAS SANCTIFIED US" – The first Hebrew word used here is "asher," which is the root word for "ashrei," which means happy and fortunate. The second word is "Kid'shanu," which is the same word used for "betrothal." The root word kadosh means "holy," and a Biblically permitted marriage between two people is a sanctified union. Here we are expressing our joy and gratitude that God has chosen us as His "partner," and "betrothed us" with His Torah. Our relationship with God is like that of a marriage, and the Torah and all its mitzvot are what bind us together.

"WITH HIS COMMANDMENTS" – How is this relationship between the Jewish people and God actualized and fulfilled? Through the fulfillment of the mitzvot of the Torah. God is concerned with our well-being. He has given us commandments so that we can build a relationship with Him. As in a marriage, each party has a responsibility to the other. For Jews, this is expressed by observing the mitzvot of the Torah. For God, it is to sanctify and protect the Jewish people.

"AND COMMANDED US CONCERNING..." – Finally, to the mitzvah at hand. On the personal level, God is speaking to the Jewish people. We have a direct, special, and personal relationship with Him, and through this mitzvah, we are now connecting with God, bringing additional holiness onto ourselves and into the world.

Each blessing then concludes with a specific phrase describing the mitzvah to be performed, or earlier (before the words "Who has sanctified us"), with the food type to be eaten. By meditating on the inner meaning of blessings, we can readily see why Jews have always said these blessings with great care and concentration. It contains the entire story of our purpose here on earth.

THE BLESSINGS OVER FOOD

Concerning food, there are six different blessings that are recited, according to their type. They are divided into the following categories (in order of food importance):

1. *Hamotzi*: Over bread or similar products (rolls, bagels, matzah, pita, etc.).

2. *Mezonot*: Over cakes, cookies, pasta, pretzels (items that are not bread, but made from wheat, barley, rye, oat, or spelt).

3. *Hagafen*: Over drinking wine or grape juice.

4. *Ha-Aytz*: Over eating any tree-grown fruits (apples, oranges, pears, plums, etc.) and certain nuts.

5. *Ha-Adama*: Over eating any earth-grown vegetables (tomatoes, peppers, cucumbers, lettuce, etc.) and legumes.

6. *Shehakol*: Over eating meat, chicken, fish, eggs, cheese, mushrooms, as well as all liquids for drinking, except wine or grape juice.

DOING IT RIGHT

The laws of the "Blessings of Enjoyment" are complex and very detailed; they cannot possibly be fully covered here. We suggest that you buy or borrow a book on this topic

Here are some basics to get you started:

- Blessings must be recited before eating or drinking kosher food and beverages.

- The six different blessings over food are based on the type of food consumed (i.e., bread, vegetables, cheese, meat, water, wine, etc.).

- Blessings are required even when eating a small amount of food.

- It is preferable to recite blessings in their original Hebrew, but some *Halachic* (Jewish legal) authorities hold that you may recite them in any language you understand.

- Once you recite the blessing, you should not talk or interrupt until you take a bite of the food or a sip of the drink you made the blessing over.

- Never recite a blessing unnecessarily, since it is forbidden to recite God's name without reason.

- Before reciting the blessing over bread, the hands must be washed ritually (see *"Hamotzi"* blessing below).

- When eating several types of food, the blessings are recited based on the food types, in the following order: bread, other baked goods (cakes, cookies), wine or grape juice, fruits and certain nuts, vegetables and legumes, meat, dairy, eggs, and all other drinks.

- When eating several types of food, and one of them is bread, the blessing over bread is recited first and exempts the need to recite other blessings during the same meal (except the blessing for drinking wine or grape juice, and over certain desserts).

- After you've finished eating or drinking, recite the appropriate "Grace After Meals" found in the prayer book (there are three kinds: over bread and meals, over snacks, and over drinks).

- *"Amein"* (Amen; "it's true" or "we are in agreement") is said after hearing someone complete a blessing.

1. Hamotzi — הַמּוֹצִיא

OVER BREAD OR SIMILAR PRODUCTS MADE FROM FLOUR AND WATER

(ROLLS, BAGELS, MATZAH, PITA, ETC.)

Before a Jew eats bread or any bread product, he is required to wash his hands ritually. This important *mitzvah* (commandment) is called *"Netilat Yadayim"* (washing the hands). Similar to the person who ritually washes his hands before praying, this mitzvah helps us properly prepare for the honor of consuming God's food, and in turn, elevates the entire meal. By properly preparing ourselves, we clearly differentiate between mankind and animals. We also make it clear to all that this meal is from God, and the table is an altar upon and through which we acquire the energies needed to serve Him.

The genesis of this mitzvah comes from the service of the *Kohanim* (priests) in the Holy Temple in Jerusalem. In those days, the Israelites brought an obligatory gift of their first wheat, wine, and olive oil harvest. This gift was called *teruma*. It could only be consumed by a kohein who had washed and purified his hands in a prescribed manner. Of the three harvest foods (wheat, wine, and olive oil), we generally only touch bread with our bare hands while eating. Therefore, the mitzvah of washing is required before eating bread.

Today, we continue to perform this mitzvah to remind us of the purity and holiness that existed in the time of the Holy Temple; a holiness and purity that will be restored to us with the coming of our righteous Moshiach, may he come speedily in our days.

HOW TO WASH THE HANDS FOR BREAD

We ritually wash the hands for bread by pouring a large cup of water over each hand three times, reciting a blessing, and completely drying our hands. The procedure is as follows:

1) Remove any rings.

2) While holding a large cup in your right hand, fill it with at least 3.5 fluid ounces of room temperature water (not too cold, not too hot).

3) Transfer the cup to your left hand, and pour over your whole right hand (many have the custom to pour three times).

4) Transfer it to your right hand, and pour over your whole left hand (many have the custom to pour three times).

5) Rub your hands together and recite the following blessing:

I find that washing before eating bread slows me down and helps me realize that there is sanctity in food

RACHEL J., AGE 44
TUCSON, AZ

בָּרוּךְ אַתָּה יְיָ, אֱלֹהֵינוּ מֶלֶךְ הָעוֹלָם, אֲשֶׁר קִדְּשָׁנוּ בְּמִצְוֹתָיו,
וְצִוָּנוּ, עַל נְטִילַת יָדָיִם:

Böruch atöh adonöy elohaynu melech hö-olöm, asher kid'shönu b'mitzvosöv,
v'tzivönu al n'tilas yödö-yim.

Blessed are You, Lord our God, King of the universe, Who has sanctified us with His commandments,
and commanded us concerning the washing of the hands.

6) Dry your hands. Do not talk until you recite the blessing below and have eaten a piece of bread.

7) After your hands are completely dry, take a piece of bread in your right hand and recite the following blessing:

בָּרוּךְ אַתָּה יְיָ, אֱלֹהֵינוּ מֶלֶךְ הָעוֹלָם,
הַמּוֹצִיא לֶחֶם מִן הָאָרֶץ:

Böruch atöh adonöy, elohaynu melech hö-olöm, hamo-tzi lechem min hö-öretz.

Blessed are You, Lord our God, King of the universe , Who brings forth bread from the earth.

It is customary to dip the first piece of bread eaten in salt. This is an additional reminder of the sacrifices on the altar which were offered with salt.

2. Mezonot – מְזוֹנוֹת

OVER CAKES, COOKIES, PASTA, PRETZELS (ITEMS THAT ARE NOT BREAD,
BUT MADE FROM WHEAT, BARLEY, RYE, OAT, OR SPELT).

בָּרוּךְ אַתָּה יְיָ, אֱלֹהֵינוּ מֶלֶךְ הָעוֹלָם,
בּוֹרֵא מִינֵי מְזוֹנוֹת:

Böruch atöh adonöy, elohaynu melech hö-olöm, bo-ray mee-nay m'zonos.

Blessed are You, Lord our God, King of the universe, Who creates various kinds of foods.

3. Hagafen — הַגֶּפֶן
OVER WINE OR GRAPE JUICE

בָּרוּךְ אַתָּה יְיָ, אֱלֹהֵינוּ מֶלֶךְ הָעוֹלָם,
בּוֹרֵא פְּרִי הַגֶּפֶן:

Böruch atöh adonöy, elohaynu melech hö-olöm, bo-ray p'ree ha-göfen.

Blessed are You, Lord our God, King of the universe, Who creates the fruit of the vine.

142

4. Ha-Aytz – הָעֵץ

OVER TREE-GROWN FRUITS (APPLES, ORANGES, PEARS, PLUMS, ETC.)

בָּרוּךְ אַתָּה יְיָ, אֱלֹהֵינוּ מֶלֶךְ הָעוֹלָם,
בּוֹרֵא פְּרִי הָעֵץ:

Böruch atöh adonöy, elohaynu melech hö-olöm, bo-ray p'ree hö-aytz.

Blessed are You, Lord our God, King of the universe, Who creates the fruit of the tree.

5. Ha-Adama – הָאֲדָמָה

OVER EARTH-GROWN VEGETABLES
(TOMATOES, PEPPFRS, CUCUMBERS, LETTUCE, ETC. EXCEPT MUSHROOMS).

בָּרוּךְ אַתָּה יְיָ, אֱלֹהֵינוּ מֶלֶךְ הָעוֹלָם,
בּוֹרֵא פְּרִי הָאֲדָמָה:

Böruch atöh adonöy, elohaynu melech hö-olöm, bo-ray p'ree hö-adö-mö.

Blessed are You, Lord our God, King of the universe, Who creates the fruit of the earth.

6. Shehakol – שֶׁהַכֹּל

OVER MEAT, CHICKEN, FISH, CHEESE, MUSHROOMS, EGGS, AS WELL AS ALL DRINKING LIQUIDS (EXCEPT WINE OR GRAPE JUICE).

בָּרוּךְ אַתָּה יְיָ, אֱלֹהֵינוּ מֶלֶךְ הָעוֹלָם,
שֶׁהַכֹּל נִהְיָה בִּדְבָרוֹ:

Böruch atöh adonöy, elohaynu melech hö-olöm, she-hakol Nee-yö bid'vöro.

Blessed are You, Lord our God, King of the universe, by Whose word all things came to be.

BLESSINGS AFTER EATING

"You shall bless the Lord your God for the good land
which He has given you." (Deuteronomy 8:10)

Just as we are required to recite a blessing before eating, we must also recite a blessing after completing a snack or meal. These are known as "After Blessings" or "Grace After Meals." Each of the After Blessings must be recited as soon as we finish eating or drinking, before the food begins to digest (i.e., within approximately 72 minutes), and in the same place as we have eaten.

Our Sages state that we should be as careful reciting the After Blessings as reciting the Blessings Before Eating. For when we are hungry, it is easy to remember God and praise Him for the food and nourishment. But once we have satisfied our hunger, it is far too easy to forget how truly dependant we are on His goodness.

There are three kinds of After Blessings:

1) After eating at least 1 ounce of bread (or similar baked products made from flour and water) — i.e., you recited the blessing of Hamotzi. This blessing is known as "Grace After Meals," also referred to as *"bentching,"* (Yiddish for blessing), or *"Bircat Ha-mazon,"* (Hebrew for "Grace After Meals").

   The Grace contains several paragraphs, plus special inserts to be recited on Shabbat, Jewish holidays, and *Rosh Chodesh* (the beginning of a new month).

If three or more Jewish males over the age of thirteen are present, a special prefatory prayer is said. All of these blessings can be found in a traditional prayer book or *"bentchers"* (Yiddish for Grace After Meal booklets).

2) After eating at least 1 ounce of a snack, or drinking at least 3.5 ounces of wine or grape juice (i.e., you've recited the blessing of *Mezonos*, *Hagafen*, or *Ha-aytz* before eating). This blessing is known as *"Al Ha-Michyah,"* or *"Me-Ein Shalosh."* It is an abbreviated version of the complete "Grace After Meals" said after eating bread.

   This "mini-grace" is recited after eating foods made from the five grains (wheat, barley, rye, oats, and spelt). This includes all baked items that are not bread (cakes, cookies, pasta, pretzels, etc.). Additionally, it is recited after drinking wine or grape juice, and/or eating any of the five "fruits of bounty" with which the Land of Israel is blessed (i.e., grapes, figs, pomegranates, olives, and dates). If one ate from any of the above three categories, or combined any of them, he inserts specific words acknowledging each type, as outlined in prayer books.

3) After eating meat, chicken, fish, or cheese, as well as drinking liquids (except wine or grape juice) (i.e., you recited the blessing of *Shehakol*). This blessing is known as *"Borei Nefashot,"* and is the shortest of all three blessings.

ABBREVIATED GRACE

There is a general grace recited by very small children. Some Rabbis suggest that adults who are just beginning to read Hebrew recite this grace until they are familiar with the Hebrew language and words of the full Grace After Meals.

בְּרִיךְ רַחֲמָנָא, אֱלָהָנָא, מַלְכָּא דְעָלְמָא, מָרֵא דְהַאי פִּתָּא׃

Brich racha-mönö, elö-hönö, mal'kö d'öl'mö, mörö d'hai pitö.

Blessed is the Lord our God, King of the universe, Master of this bread.

Today, however, many prayer books and *bentchers* have all the necessary blessings in English; some even have line-by-line English transliterations of the Hebrew words (see our own "Companion Series"), making it easier to practice and recite them in their original Hebrew. So really, there is no compelling reason to use the children's abridged prayer. Instead, we suggest that you become familiar with the "real thing."

TODAY'S ACTION
Take the "Kosher Shopping Quiz" and learn about buying kosher food.

DAY 16

Shopping
Kosher

egardless of whether you live in an area with a large Jewish population, or if you are the lone Jewish family in your city, you can readily find thousands of kosher food products on your supermarket or grocery shelves. It's no wonder that many say we are living in the "golden age" of availability of kosher food. The fact is, almost every name-brand manufacturer produces many kosher certified products. You'll find packaged and ready-to-eat kosher meats, fish, dairy products, cakes, cookies, candies, condiments, baking supplies, and much more. We estimate that you can find kosher versions (or at least close substitutes) of nearly 95 to 98 percent of the present contents of your pantry and fridge. What's more, these brands will be equal to, if not better than, the non-kosher brands in both taste and quality.

If you live in a large metropolitan area, there is an added advantage; typically large cities have one or more kosher certified butcher shops and bakeries that provide consumers with fresh kosher meats and delicious baked goods.

KOSHER IS NOT EXPENSIVE

Some consumers erroneously believe that kosher foods carry a price premium, much like a "kosher tax." In today's competitive marketplace, the vast majority of kosher food products cost the same as similar non-kosher foods in the same category, and sometimes may even be less expensive.

The main exception can be found with meat and dairy products. These can be priced ten or fifteen percent higher than similar non-kosher products. This is because manufacturers have the additional expenses of obtaining kosher ingredients, hiring expert Rabbinical supervision, and producing and packaging the food items to strict kosher standards. If you live in a small town, you may also have to pay a premium to cover the cost of trucking kosher food to your store. In either case, the slightly higher cost is by far offset by the immeasurable spiritual and physical rewards one receives from observing the *mitzvah* (commandment) of kosher.

THE KOSHER SHOPPING QUIZ

How much do you know about shopping kosher? Take the following quiz and see for yourself:

Answer true or false?

1) THE LABEL HAS A PICTURE OF A MENORAH OR JEWISH STAR, SO IT'S PROBABLY KOSHER.

2) THE LABEL SAYS IT CONTAINS 100 PERCENT NATURAL INGREDIENTS, SO IT'S KOSHER.

3) THE PRODUCT IS INTRINSICALLY KOSHER (I.E., PEAS, TUNA, ORGANIC BREAD, ETC.), SO I DON'T HAVE TO WORRY.

4) THE INGREDIENTS DO NOT LIST ANYTHING THAT IS OBVIOUSLY NON-KOSHER, SO IT'S KOSHER.

5) THE BUTCHER OR BAKER HAS A SIGN IN THE WINDOW THAT SAYS "KOSHER," SO IT'S KOSHER.

6) I SAW "SO-AND-SO" EAT THE SAME FOOD, SO IT MUST BE KOSHER.

The correct answer to all of the above questions is FALSE.

Surprised? Let's examine each item from the quiz to get a better understanding about shopping kosher the right way.

1) "The label has a picture of a menorah or Jewish star, so it's probably kosher."

This is a common mistake. Nothing in the United States trade law prohibits a company from putting a menorah, or for that matter, any other Jewish symbol on their food packaging. Moreover, displaying a Jewish picture does not make the contents kosher any more than a Rabbi "blessing the food" does. Either the food, including the ingredients and equipment it's prepared on, meets kosher standards, or it does not. Unless the product has a reliable kosher certification symbol, it cannot be assumed to be kosher.

2) The label says it contains 100 percent natural ingredients, so it's kosher.

Natural or "organic" products may come from non-kosher origins or contain tiny insects or worms that make them non-kosher. Some products might be manufactured on non-kosher equipment, or contain non-kosher oils, processing agents, or release agents. You can never truly tell by just reading the ingredients panel on the package, especially since by U.S. trade law, manufacturers are not required to list components that are less than 2 percent of the whole product (a ratio that according to kosher law often renders the entire product non-kosher should the ingredient be from a non-kosher source).

3) The product is intrinsically kosher (i.e., green peas, tuna, organic bread, etc.), so I don't have to worry.

Sophisticated food production techniques, plus advances in ingredient formulations can affect even intrinsically "kosher" products. For example, the food item could be enhanced by non-kosher flavorings, coloring, or preservatives that can render the "naturally kosher" non-kosher. As another example, a can of "natural" tuna might have small bits of non-kosher fish mixed in with it (very common in factories without meticulous kosher supervision).

Additionally, consider the pots, pans, steamers, and ovens that are used to produce intrinsically kosher or "natural" foods that are also often used for non-kosher product runs, rendering what appears to be a "naturally" kosher food completely non-kosher.

4) The ingredients do not list anything that is obviously non-kosher, so it's kosher.

By now you should be able to answer this one yourself. Many ingredients (i.e., "home-style" sauces or "special" seasonings) on labels may have components that are non-kosher, rendering the product it was added to non-kosher in turn. In addition, formulas often change due to ingredient availability and cost. For this reason, reliable kosher certifying agencies maintain a constantly updated database of thousands of ingredients. The database enables the certifying Rabbi to identify the individual components of all ingredients in order to ensure kosher continuity throughout the food production process.

5) The butcher or baker has a sign in the window that says "Kosher," so it's kosher.

A sign alone does not make an item kosher. Unless the sign is from a well-known and noted kosher certifying agency you need to ask, "According to whose standards is this kosher?"

The following story will illustrate this point. A kosher-observant tourist enters what appears to be a kosher deli. He sees someone standing behind the counter, but because of his non-religious

When I learned that any ingredient that is less then 2 percent of the product does not have to be listed on the ingredients panel, I realized how alert I must be.

RIVKAH D., AGE 42
FT. LAUDERDALE, FL

appearance, the tourist isn't sure if he is in the right place. So he asks, "Do you serve kosher food here?" The man behind the counter says yes, then points to an old, worn picture of a pious-looking Rabbi on the wall and says, "Don't worry. That man was my grandfather. You can be assured the food here is kosher." The tourist replies, "If your *grandfather* was standing behind the counter and *your picture* was on the wall, then I'd feel more comfortable about the kosher standards of this place!"

Indeed, any assurances of "kosher" are only as good as the reliability of the person or people making the claim.

6) I saw "so-and-so" eat the same food, so it must be kosher.

People and their standards change, and sometimes you just don't know how much the person you saw is committed to keeping kosher. Furthermore, manufacturers and ingredients change, so the product may indeed have been kosher before, but is not now.

The point is, a kosher consumer must be an educated consumer. Before you buy any item, make sure to look for a kosher symbol (see next chapter) and any designation (i.e., if it is pareve, dairy [often has the letters "D" after the kosher symbol], or made on dairy equipment [often has the letters "DE" after the kosher symbol], etc.).

DAY 17

Kosher Supervision
& Certification

With the commercialization of food production, kosher consumers are constantly challenged to ensure that the items they purchase are indeed kosher, meaning that the item has maintained true "kosher continuity" throughout the entire production and packaging process. Today, major food companies use ingredients from all over the world, producing foods in different plants, often using the same production lines to run kosher and non-kosher products at different times.

As a result, determining the kosher status of any single item has become increasingly difficult. This challenge has given rise to the "Kosher Certifying Agency," comprised of Rabbis who are experts in kosher dietary law, as well as *mashgichim* (Hebrew for "supervisors"), who monitor food production and preparation at each facility.

Reliable kosher certifying agencies also maintain close ties with food chemists, scientists, and raw material producers, in order to understand modern food production methods and to know whom to ask when technical questions arise.

Today, there are scores of kosher agencies with varying levels of kosher adherence and protection. These agencies certify food manufacturers, restaurants, butcher's shops, bakeries, and commercial food establishments such as caterers, hospital kitchens, etc. In addition to these certifying agencies, large cities often have their own *Vaad HaKashrut* (certifying board of kosher supervision), comprised of local Rabbis. Many synagogues and communities also maintain their own kosher organizations.

At the end of the day, everyone involved in the responsible task of kosher certification must be deeply religious and God-fearing, have a broad knowledge of kosher dietary laws and modern food production technologies, and a profound sense of responsibility to the public they serve.

THE KOSHER DETECTIVE

There are so many ways food can lose its kosher status that there is no certain way to know if the final product is kosher without meticulous supervision. Therefore, reputable kosher certification is absolutely imperative when purchasing processed and packaged foods sold by grocers, delis, restaurants, caterers, and so forth.

Furthermore, any time food is prepared or handled, especially by someone who isn't kosher observant himself, it requires proof of its ongoing kosher status. This is because it is a fundamental kosher principal that it is imprudent to expect someone who doesn't care about kosher to follow the letter of the law (and beyond) with the same care as one who is strictly kosher. For all the above reasons, an educated kosher shopper must be a "kosher detective" to ensure that the product he is purchasing or consuming is truly kosher, and that the kosher certifying agency is legitimate.

This task is easily enough accomplished by making sure the product is sealed by the factory, and by looking for a kosher symbol of any of the "big four" kosher certifying agencies on the packaging (see following page) before placing it in your shopping cart; or by requesting to see a valid, unexpired kosher certificate at restaurants and in other food establishments where food is sold in open or unsealed packages. You will find that checking food labels for a kosher symbol soon becomes second nature.

WHO CAN GIVE "KOSHER CERTIFICATION"?

As mentioned above, a proper kosher certifying agency is organized and run by competent religious Rabbis who have experience with modern food production and are experts in kosher dietary law. Today, there are many reliable kosher certification agencies around, yet the consumer should be aware that a small number sadly play fast and loose with kosher law at the expense of the kosher consumer.

Since anyone can create a logo that can look like an authentic kosher symbol, or print the plain letter "K" (purportedly for "kosher") on the package, consumers must educate themselves about the various kosher symbols and the people behind them.

157

HOW DOES KOSHER CERTIFICATION WORK?

At the request of a manufacturer or food purveyor, a kosher certifying agency will assign an expert Rabbi to inspect the production plant (or in the case of a restaurant, caterer, or other food purveyor, their kitchen and operation), review the food recipes, ingredients, production methods, and train the staff on kosher dietary requirements.

The agency will then trace every single ingredient used back to its component parts — an enormously complicated task as ingredients are often complex composites of several, or even hundreds of other food and chemical components — to ensure they are kosher, and make sure the equipment the food will be prepared on is kosher (or properly kosherized) as well. Once the entire process is approved, a trained religious kosher expert is sent to monitor each "production run" to ensure that all kosher-related requirements are being meticulously followed. If all goes according to plan, the agent and the agency sign off on each approved batch of production and the company is permitted to print the certifying agency's trademarked kosher symbol on the food package, or display it on a sign in their store.

THE WORLD OF KOSHER SYMBOLS

As mentioned earlier, there are hundreds of kosher certifying agencies around the world, many having their own symbol or logo. Therefore, it is nearly impossible to know who stands behind every kosher guarantee. Just because a logo has Hebrew words or looks like a Jewish symbol does not mean it is from a reliable kosher certifying agency. Fortunately, the majority of kosher products today bear a symbol from one of four major and highly respected kosher certifying agencies. These agencies have trademarked their symbols so that they can only be printed on packages with permission by the issuing agency. To protect the kosher consumer, and its own reputation, the agency will make sure that any unauthorized products sold displaying their kosher symbol are immediately recalled and withdrawn from the marketplace.

Pronounced: O-U The Union of Orthodox Jewish Congregations 11 Broadway New York, NY 10004 212-563-4000 www.OU.org	*Pronounced:* O-K OK Kosher Certification 391 Troy Avenue Brooklyn, NY 11213 718-756-7500 www.OK.org
Pronounced: Star-K Star-K Kosher Certification 122 Slade Avenue, Suite 300 Baltimore, MD 21208 410-484-4110 www.Star-K.org	*Pronounced:* Chof-K KOF-K Kosher Supervision 201 The Plaza Teaneck, NJ 07666 201-837-0500 www.Kof-K.org

If a packaged item has any of the kosher symbols above, you can buy it with confidence. If the logo looks different from the "big four," find out who is behind the symbol. You can try looking it up online, calling your local Orthodox Rabbi, or try calling any of the certification agencies above for information.

THE PLAIN LETTER "K"

Often, manufacturers print the letter "K" (purportedly for "kosher") on food packages, indicating that according to *their* estimate, the item is kosher. With no expert Rabbinical supervision and many cases of abuses occurring over the years, the designation of "K" has become meaningless and should never be relied upon alone, unless another well-known kosher symbol is printed on the package, or you know specifically that this particular product is kosher.

One should also be careful not to mistaken the commonly used ®, ©, or ™ as kosher symbols. (Children should be made aware of this as well).

REPACKAGED FOOD ITEMS

Sometimes a store or supermarket might repackage a food item that they purchased in bulk (i.e., candies, meat, chicken, etc.) into smaller packages and print their own private brand labels. This practice is not without its flaws, for not all store employees are familiar with the various kosher issues, and mistakes are unfortunately rampant. Unless a *mashgiach* (expert religious kosher supervisor) from the kosher certifying agency oversees the repackaging and personally seals each and every package, you cannot assume the item is kosher, regardless of what's printed on it.

TODAY'S ACTION
Visit your local
kosher butcher,
baker, and grocer.

DAY 18

The Butcher, Baker
& Grocer

*J*ust as large industrial food manufacturers require expert kosher supervision, the same can be said for any kosher food establishment. Experience has shown in too many situations that non-kosher food can be easily sold as kosher by accident. Therefore, when you shop at the butcher's shop, bakery, or any other food establishment and buy a food item that is not factory-sealed or packaged by the manufacturer, make sure the store itself has active, independent kosher supervision from a respected kosher certification agency. It's the only sure way to know that the food you are purchasing and eating is truly kosher.

THE BUTCHER

A kosher butcher must be a devoutly religious person who is exceptionally knowledgeable in the kosher dietary laws and have the utmost integrity. Often problems arise concerning the kosher status of an incoming shipment or even just a single tray of meat. You must be able to trust that the butcher is not swayed by potential monetary loss or gain, to cut any kosher corners.

A sign at a butcher that simply states "Kosher Meats" is empty and meaningless today. A trustworthy kosher butcher should welcome independent kosher supervision from a recognized and respected kosher certification agency, and proudly display their kosher certificate.

When purchasing kosher meats at a supermarket, make sure the product is in its original factory packaging (not repackaged) and has a kosher symbol that is printed on the actual package (not merely a sticker).

As an additional protective measure, many large cuts of kosher meat and chicken have a small metal clip-seal that is attached at the factory called a *"plumba."* This definitely helps ensure that non-kosher meat was not substituted. Make sure to look for it. Some smaller meat or chicken cuts may not bear a plumba (for example, filleted chicken breasts, meat cubes, etc.). In such cases, only purchase them if packaged in their original factory-sealed packaging, with the respective kosher certification clearly marked.

THE BAKER

Due to the variety of ingredients, the nature of the equipment used, and additional concerns regarding baking kosher bread (see "Day 23"), all bakeries require independent kosher supervision from a recognized and respected kosher certification agency. One may purchase baked goods found in local supermarkets or stores if they have a reliable kosher symbol on the package. One should also look for the marking "PAS YISRAEL" (or in Hebrew, פת ישראל) on the bag or package. Without this marking, the baked goods should not be assumed to be Pas Yisrael.

THE GROCER

All uncut fruits and vegetables, as well as unprocessed nuts and eggs, may be purchased at any grocery or market. All pre-packaged foods must bear an acceptable kosher symbol on the package. There are a few exceptions to this rule, such as foods that are known to pose no or little kosher concerns (for example, frozen vegetables, because the equipment they are prepared on are known to be used solely to process raw vegetables [as of this printing]). But for the most part, always look for a reliable kosher symbol on the food package before putting the item into your cart.

Some grocers sell pre-cut fruits and vegetables, or have a fish department where they grind fish at your request. Unless the store has active kosher supervision as evidenced by the display of a current (unexpired) kosher certificate from a reliable certifying agency, or you see a *mashgiach* (expert religious kosher supervisor) from a reliable kosher agency on the premises, you must make sure that the knives and equipment are used exclusively by that department and not washed together with other non-kosher utensils. (Purchasing fresh fish poses its own concerns, see "Day 21").

TODAY'S ACTION
Replace the meats and poultry in your fridge with kosher varieties.

DAY 19

Meat, Poultry & Meat Products

*Y*f bread is the "staff of life," meat completes the sandwich! Festive Shabbat and Jewish holiday meals would not be the same without meat and poultry. For meat to be considered kosher, there are many laws detailing their proper slaughter, inspection, preparation, and consumption. From simple ground beef, to an obscure component in a food flavoring or ingredient, the kosher consumer needs to know what's meaty, where the meat came from, and whether or not it is kosher.

WHAT IS CONSIDERED "MEATY"?

Meat, poultry, and any derivative product is considered meaty or *fleishig* (Yiddish for "meaty"). When even a small amount of meaty product is added to another food, the other food also becomes meaty. This is why people have special pots, pans, dishes, silverware, and utensils for preparing and eating meaty foods.

KOSHER ANIMALS

Kosher animals have completely split hooves and chew their cud, and are slaughtered, inspected, and prepared according to Jewish law.

Common kosher animals are:

- Cows
- Goats
- Lamb/Sheep
- Deer

NON-KOSHER ANIMALS

Any animal that does not have completely split hooves and does not chew its cud is not kosher. This also includes kosher animals that have not been properly slaughtered, inspected, or prepared according to Jewish law, as well as those found to have broken bones or certain diseases after they've been slaughtered.

Common non-kosher animals are:

- Pigs
- Camels
- Horses
- Rabbits

FOWL & POULTRY

The Torah forbids twenty-four predatory and scavenger birds. While the Torah does not list specific signs to tell which birds are kosher, we have a tradition specifying those birds that are universally accepted as kosher.

Common kosher birds are:
- Chickens (domesticated)
- Certain Ducks
- Turkeys
- Cornish hens
- Certain Geese

Common non-kosher birds are:
- Eagles
- Hawks
- Pelicans
- Swans
- Ostrich
- Owls
- Storks
- Vultures

THE PROHIBITION AGAINST CRUELTY TO ANIMALS

The Torah permits the consumption of meat only when observing its protective dictates, including the prohibition against cruelty to animals. Thus we find laws in the Torah governing the proper care and raising of animals.

In Genesis (9:2-4) we find a command given to the sons of Noah, the only remnants of the human race surviving the Great Flood:

"All the birds of the skies, everything that ruminates upon the ground, and all the fish in the sea, they have been given into your hand. Every moving thing that lives shall be yours to eat. Like the green vegetation, I have given you everything. But do not eat the flesh of an animal or its blood while it is still alive."

Later on, God gives the Jewish people the kosher dietary laws (Leviticus 11:4-5). These laws describe which animals are permitted, and provide very specific guidelines on their slaughter, inspection, and preparation. For example, a *shochet* (ritual slaughterer) cannot kill an animal by poking, piercing, or shooting. Nor may a Jew kill for sport. In addition to remaining true to the Torah's requirements, observing these laws enables the Jew to attain a greater level of spiritual refinement.

THE SHOCHET — RITUAL SLAUGHTERER

A qualified shochet is proficient in the laws and practical aspects of kosher ritual slaughter and has been tested and certified as such by a respected *Halachic* (Jewish legal) rabbinical authority. After visually inspecting the animal to make sure it is not diseased, he slaughters it in the swiftest way possible. The *chalef* (specially designated knife) that the shochet uses must be extremely sharp; even a tiny nick makes it unusable for kosher meat. In addition, there are several strict requirements that the shochet must follow for the slaughtered meat to be considered kosher. Omitting any of these steps renders the meat from that animal non-kosher.

Over the centuries, various animal-rights and anti-Semitic groups have tried to have legislation enacted to ban *Shechita* (the kosher form of slaughter), but they have rarely succeeded. Shechita has consistently been shown to be a very sensitive and effective form of slaughter.

KOSHER MEAT CUTS

Only certain parts of kosher animals are permitted to be consumed; these include the front section until the twelfth rib. (Biblically, certain veins must be removed and it is extremely difficult to remove them beyond the twelfth rib.) All remaining sections are sold to non-kosher butchers.

Permissible meat cuts are:

- Neck (beef, veal, lamb)
- Foreshank (beef, veal)
- Chuck (beef)
- Short plate (beef)
- Shank (lamb)
- Shoulder (beef, veal, lamb)
- Brisket (beef)
- Rib (beef, veal, lamb)
- Breast (veal, lamb)

Other parts such as tongue, liver, or sweetbread require special preparation and should only be purchased from a reliable kosher butcher. For those that had to ask, yes, eyeballs, earlobes, and hooves are all kosher, but as you probably guessed, they are not widely sought after for their appeal.

All parts of poultry and fowl are considered kosher. Chicken and beef liver, however, must be roasted over a fire to remove all blood before one can consume them.

PREPARING MEAT FOR CONSUMPTION

In order for meat and fowl to be fit for consumption, they must be prepared according to Jewish law. This includes:

1. Slaughter by a spiritually sensitive and expert Jewish shochet.

2. Internal inspection for defective organs by a trained Rabbi.

3. Soaking and salting the meat to draw out all blood.

4. Removal of certain fats and veins (i.e., sciatic nerve in the hind quarters, etc.).

5. Expert kosher supervision up until you purchase the product.

If even *one* of the above requirements is omitted, the meat is non-kosher and can render any kosher food it comes in contact with as non-kosher as well.

MIXING MEAT & DAIRY

It is Biblically forbidden to cook, bake, roast, fry, or steam meaty and dairy foods together. This prohibition includes eating combinations of meat and dairy (such as a cheeseburger) or deriving any benefit from a meat and dairy combination (i.e., through commerce, serving them to one's animals or pets, etc.). Therefore, separate utensils are used for preparing, serving, and eating dairy foods.

A person who eats meat or meaty foods must wait six hours before eating dairy. Different customs exist regarding the exact amount of time one needs to wait — ask your kosher expert about your own community's custom. (See "Day 5" regarding the waiting period for children.)

Without proper care and attention in the kitchen, the prohibition of mixing meat and dairy can be easily transgressed. For example, if a person is cooking a meaty food and adds a dairy product or uses a dairy utensil by mistake, or something dairy accidentally falls into the pot; the food, pot, plus all utensils used become non-kosher. The food may have to be discarded, and the pot and utensils properly kosherized before they can be used again for kosher food.

There are some circumstances where the food, pot, and utensils are not rendered non-kosher. For example, if a tiny amount of dairy falls into (or was mistakenly added to) a pot of beef or chicken soup. If it is not recognizable, does not add taste or modify the product, and the ratio is 1 part (or less) to 60 parts, then the smaller part is said to be "nullified" and the food remains kosher. (Be aware that this is not applicable in all situations, nor with all foods.) Therefore, when you encounter a confusing or questionable scenario in your kitchen travails, call an Orthodox Rabbi or your kosher expert and run the scenario by him. Sometimes, a particular set of circumstances will have a simple remedy.

It took me a while to get used to keeping things separate. Practicing before I kosherized really helped.

ELIZABETH K., AGE 29
DAVENPORT, IA

WHAT IS GLATT KOSHER?

Today, it is very common to hear or see the term GLATT KOSHER used in reference to kosher meat, meat products, and even food establishments (i.e., "our restaurant is Glatt kosher"). This has come to mean that the meat is kosher at the "highest level" possible.

The term "Glatt" is Yiddish for "perfectly smooth," and it refers to the lungs of the animal. As mentioned earlier, after an animal is slaughtered, the shochet or Rabbi inspects the animal, including the lungs, to make sure there are no diseases or problems that cause the animal to lose its kosher status. Sometimes, certain small adhesions found on the lungs are still technically acceptable as kosher. If the lungs are found to be exceptionally smooth and healthy, they are "glatt," in other words, kosher without any doubt. Thus, glatt has popularly come to mean "kosher without compromises" or without resorting to Halachic leniencies.

BLESSING BEFORE & AFTER EATING MEAT OR POULTRY

If consumed without bread, the blessing recited is *"Shehakol."* The after-blessing is *"Boray Nefashot"* (see "Day 15").

DAY 20

Milk & Dairy Products

*T*he Land of Israel is frequently referred to as the "Land of Milk and Honey," referring to God's eternal blessings for its earthly bounty. Indeed, milk, butter, and cheese have traditionally been associated with good times and fortune. The kosher dietary laws permit the consumption of all dairy products that come from a kosher animal that have had the milking and preparation supervised by a religious Jew. To remain kosher, the dairy product must not contain any non-kosher additives or ingredients, nor be eaten or cooked with meat or meaty products or utensils. Therefore, during any manufacturing and processing of any dairy goods, expert kosher supervision is required to ensure that non-kosher milk or additives are not added, and that all equipment, including vats, pasteurizers, transporting tankers, etc., have been properly washed and kosherized prior to each kosher dairy run.

Many dairy products, especially hard cheeses, contain enzymes, stabilizers, or flavor enhancers that originate from non-kosher meat sources. It is therefore imperative to check for a kosher symbol from a recognized kosher certification agency on the packaging before purchasing any dairy product, especially for cheese.

WHAT IS CONSIDERED "DAIRY"?
Milk and all derivative food products are considered "dairy," or *milchig* (Yiddish for dairy). These include butter, hard- and soft cheeses, yogurts, etc. When even a small amount of dairy product is added to another food, the affected food becomes dairy.

MIXING DAIRY & MEAT
It is Biblically forbidden to cook, bake, roast, fry, or steam dairy and meaty products together. This prohibition includes eating combinations of dairy and meat (such as a cheeseburger), or deriving any benefit from a dairy and meat combination (i.e., through commerce). Therefore, separate utensils are used for preparing, serving, and eating dairy foods.

A person who eats dairy foods must wait thirty minutes (pious Jews wait an hour) before eating anything meaty, and six hours for certain aged, hard cheeses. (See "Day 5" regarding the waiting period for children).

Similar to the precautions mentioned earlier with meat ("Day 19"), without proper care and attention the prohibition of mixing dairy and meat can be easily transgressed in the kitchen. For example, if a person is cooking a dairy food and some meat product is used, or accidentally falls into the pot; or if a meaty utensil is used by mistake, the food, pot, plus all utensils used are now possibly non-kosher. The prepared food may have to be discarded, and the pot and utensils properly kosherized before they can be used again for kosher food.

There are some circumstances where the food, pot, and utensils are not rendered non-kosher. For example, if a tiny amount of meaty substance falls onto (or was mistakenly added to) a pot of dairy soup. If it is not recognizable, does not add taste or modify the product, and the ratio is 1 part (or less) to 60 parts, then the smaller part is said to be "nullified" and the food remains kosher. (Be aware that this is not applicable in all situations, nor with all foods.) Therefore, when you encounter a confusing or questionable scenario in your kitchen travails, call an Orthodox Rabbi or your kosher expert and run the scenario by him. Sometimes, a particular set of circumstances will have a simple remedy.

CHALAV YISRAEL, CHALAV AKUM/STAM

These are several Hebrew terms to know when buying kosher dairy products. They refer to the level of kosher supervision provided at the time of milking.

- CHALAV YISRAEL — Chalav is Hebrew for "milk." Chalav Yisrael is milk that was supervised by a Jew from the time of milking all the way to the final packaging. Chalav Yisrael is not merely a *chumra* (added stringency) but a requirement of Jewish law.

- CHALAV AKUM — "Gentile milk." Refers to milk from a milking that was not supervised by a Jew. It is considered non-kosher and should not be consumed.

- CHALAV STAM — Common in developed countries, refers to milk from a milking of a kosher animal that was not supervised by a Jew, but instead relies on certain Halachic leniencies allowing governmental oversight to ensure that milk from non-kosher animals was not added to the kosher milk. Products made from Chalav Stam must still bear a reliable kosher symbol certifying that the rest of the processing (pasteurization, any additives and ingredients, stabilizers, etc.) is kosher.

All Rabbinic authorities agree that the kosher consumer's first choice should be Chalav Yisrael over Chalav Stam, for as mentioned above, Chalav Yisrael is a clear requirement of Jewish law. Furthermore, the leniency of permitting Chalav Stam was only relied upon when Chalav Yisrael products could not readily found in America in the early 1900s. Now that Chalav Yisrael is available in most cities (even if requiring some effort or additional expense), Jewish law does not permit one to rely on the leniency of Chalav Stam.

It should be noted that for spiritual and mystical reasons, pious Jews are extremely careful to only use Chalav Yisrael, and would sooner do without dairy products than rely on leniencies. Thus, they do not eat food prepared with utensils that were used for Chalav Stam. In addition to the mystical reasons for only using Chalav Yisrael milk, there still always remains the chance that without expert *Jewish* supervision at the milking, non-kosher milk may have made its way into the final product.

Finally, "government oversight" requires only random, sporadic spot-checks carried out by inspectors who know little or nothing about kosher law, and are certainly not concerned with the kosher state of the plant's equipment (vats, pasteurizer, etc.). For all these reasons, Chalav Yisrael should be everyone's first choice.

I remember my grand- father travel- ing six hours (each way!) in order to bring home Chalav Yisrael milk.

SARAH J., AGE 62
DETROIT, MI

SPECIAL DAIRY KOSHER SYMBOLS

When purchasing any type of kosher dairy product, make sure the package bears a kosher symbol from a reliable and reputable kosher certifying agency. In addition, look for the words "CHALAV YISRAEL" (or in Hebrew, חלב ישראל). All dairy products that bear a kosher symbol but do not state Chalav Yisrael should be assumed to be Chalav Stam (unless one knows for certain otherwise).

You may find products with the letter "D" (for dairy) next to the kosher symbol (i.e., OU-D or OK-D). This indicates that the product is dairy and certified kosher (but not Chalav Yisrael), and should not be used or eaten with meat. You may also find products with the letters "DE" (dairy equipment) on it (i.e., OK-DE), which generally means that non-Chalav Yisrael processing equipment was used. This tells the consumer that while the product may not be inherently "dairy" (e.g., pareve dark chocolate), it affects the product's use and consumption with meaty products for it was manufactured or cooked on dairy equipment. Furthermore, those who do no eat foods prepared on equipment that was also used for non-Chalav Yisrael products, will know not to eat foods with the "DE" designation.

OTHER DAIRY CONSIDERATIONS

- Before performing a "kosher run" of dairy products (i.e., milk, cheeses, ice-cream, chocolate milk, etc.) at a non-kosher dairy facility, all equipment must be purged of its non-kosher flavor and residue. This is done with running boiling water through the entire system. In the Western hemisphere, the boiling point of water is 212 Fahrenheit (about 100 degrees Celsius). Therefore, you need to make sure that the kosher certifying agency adheres to this standard, for there are some that permit lower temperatures (which many Halachic authorities believe not to be hot enough to effectively kosherize the equipment).

- Dairy baby formulas require kosher supervision. If none is available, you should use a kosher non-dairy formula, or ask a kosher expert for guidance.

BLESSING BEFORE & AFTER EATING DAIRY PRODUCTS

If consumed without bread, the blessing recited is "*Shehakol.*" The after-blessing is "*Boray Nefashot*" (see "Day 15").

TODAY'S ACTION
Replace the fish
and fish products
in your fridge with
kosher varieties.

DAY 21

Fish
& Fish Products

*T*he only thing more Jewish than lox and bagels is, of course, their kosher status! According to the Torah, any fish that has fins and scales is kosher; all other creatures of the sea are forbidden. Fish do not require ritual slaughter, nor soaking and salting of their meat as kosher animals do. Fish are also considered *pareve*, being neither meaty nor dairy. However, as mentioned earlier (see "Day 5"), due to health related concerns discussed in the *Talmud*, fish is not cooked or eaten with meat, but may be served a separate course in a meaty meal, using separate dishes and silverware. Some pious Jews extend this protective measure to include not eating fish and milk together either; however, most *Halachic* (Jewish legal) authorities are lenient in this matter. All authorities agree that, as with a meaty meal, it is permissible to eat fish during a dairy meal, provided it is served as a separate course on its own plates and silverware.

WHICH FISH ARE KOSHER?

As mentioned above, fish must have both fins and scales to be considered kosher. All other sea creatures, including fish with scales that cannot be removed without tearing the skin, are not kosher. Often what look like fins or scales are not; therefore, one should never assume a fish is kosher unless the particular species of fish is widely known to be kosher, or the fish in question is inspected by a kosher expert. Interestingly, the *Talmud* notes that all fish that have scales also have fins. Therefore, if one finds scales on a piece of fish, he can probably assume the fish is kosher.

Common kosher fish are:

- Carp
- Flounder
- Halibut
- Herring, Sardines
- Pike
- Tilapia
- Tuna
- Cod
- Haddock
- Hecht
- Mackerel Tuna
- Salmon
- Trout
- Whitefish

Common non-kosher fish are:

- All shellfish, including clams, crab, lobster, oyster and shrimp
- Marlin
- Shark
- Sturgeon

- Catfish
- Eel
- Octopus
- Skate
- Swordfish

PURCHASING FISH

One should only purchase fish from a kosher fish store that has active and reliable kosher supervision. This is because species substitution has become a prevalent problem in fish markets, especially when purchasing fillets, ground fish, caviar, and roe. For once the fish is filleted or processed, it is no longer possible to inspect the fish for its fins and scales. Therefore, you can only assume the fish is kosher if some of the skin is still attached and the signs recognizable, or if there was reliable kosher supervision during the processing.

If there aren't any kosher fish stores in your city, you can purchase traditionally known kosher species of fish at stores or markets that also sell non-kosher fish, but know that the knives and equipment used there are not kosher and cannot be used for cutting and preparing your kosher fish because of the absorbed fat and residue from non-kosher fish. The solution is rather simple: bring your own knife! In this case, buy a complete kosher fish with its skin still attached (so you can inspect the fins and scales), and have the fish seller scale and cut the fish with your kosher knife. Before doing so, ask to have the counter wiped with a clean cloth and a new sheet of paper laid down upon which the fish will be prepared.

CANNED FISH

Canned fish, such as tuna, must bear a kosher symbol on their package from a reliable kosher certification agency. Preferably, the agency should provide constant, full-time expert kosher supervision (not relying on sporadic spot-checks) beginning with when the fish are brought to the cannery from the sea, until the product is canned and delivered to the distributor. This thorough supervision is usually indicated next to the kosher symbol on the can's label with the words "MASHGIACH TEMIDI" (or in Hebrew, משגיח תמידי), which loosely translated from Hebrew means "constant supervision."

Canned sardines must have their skin still attached (so you can check for fins and scales) in addition to a kosher symbol on the label. Skinless canned salmon is acceptable without the extra designation of a Mashgiach Temidi, because its meat color is easily identifiable as kosher salmon. It must still, however, bear a kosher symbol on the label to ensure the rest of the processing (i.e., any flavoring, additives, or preservatives added, including heating, cooking, and packing) was strictly kosher.

All these precautions are necessary because non-kosher fish are also caught in the sailors' nets and carried into the ship's holds alongside the kosher fish. These non-kosher fish later make their way onto the kosher fish production line. Together with loose factory quality control and lax (if any) government oversight, this too often results in non-kosher fish being mixed into the final "kosher" product.

Additionally, canning processes include heating the canned fish in large vats that are also used to cook pet food containing non-kosher meat or chicken. Therefore, kosher certification is required to ensure that these vats and all other equipment used were properly cleaned and kosherized before use.

SMOKED FISH

Smoked fish requires reliable kosher supervision and must bear a kosher symbol on their package from a reliable kosher certification agency, since smoking is often done in batches together with non-kosher fish.

BLESSING BEFORE & AFTER EATING FISH

If consumed without bread, the blessing recited is *"Shehakol."* The after-blessing is *"Boray Nefashot"* (see "Day 15").

TODAY'S ACTION
Learn about
"neutral" foods
that are neither
meat nor dairy.

DAY 22

Fruits, Vegetables, Nuts, Eggs & Pareve

*P*areve means "neutral" in Hebrew, and describes all foods that are neither meaty nor dairy, and may be cooked or eaten with either one. This category includes all natural and unprocessed fruit, vegetables, nuts, legumes, grains, fish, and kosher eggs. Pareve foods in their *natural* and *unprocessed* state generally do not require kosher certification. However, once a pareve food is processed by a manufacturer in any way, it must have reliable kosher certification. The need for kosher certification on natural foods is often under-appreciated and misunderstood. Many people don't realize that natural seldom means "unprocessed."

For example, apples are often waxed so they shine, but the wax is often produced from non-kosher fats. Consider, too, the massive commercial ovens used to roast nuts or process other products. Were these same ovens previously used for pork rinds? And was the equipment properly kosherized in between? In this light it is very understandable why the kosher consumer cannot assume a food product is kosher just because the package states it is "natural."

With that said, you can generally purchase all raw fruits, vegetables, nuts, legumes, grains, and kosher eggs anywhere you wish. You should just make sure the food is truly "natural." If the food was processed in any way, the package should bear a kosher symbol from a reliable and reputable kosher certifying agency.

INSPECTING VEGETABLES, HERBS, NUTS & GRAINS FOR INSECTS OR WORMS

Before consuming or cooking vegetables, herbs, beans, and grains, keep in mind that they need to be inspected for insects and worms (which are not kosher). Leafy vegetables often have tiny insects, such as aphids, thrips, and leaf-miners on their leaves and buried in crevices (especially "organic" vegetables that are grown *sans* insecticides). In addition, certain nuts and grains (i.e., barely, beans, pasta, certain spices, and flours) attract tiny worms. Therefore, one must carefully wash and inspect vegetables and sift and inspect problem grains before using them.

Vegetables that are known to commonly have insects are:

- Artichokes
- Asparagus
- Broccoli
- Brussel sprouts
- Cabbage
- Cauliflower
- Celery
- Lettuce
- Spinach and all leafy vegetables

Leafy vegetables should be rinsed very well to remove all insects, and then inspected leaf by leaf under a bright light to make sure there are no insects remaining. Soaking the leaves first in salt-water often helps.

Vegetables such as celery or broccoli stalks can be scrubbed with a vegetable brush to help remove any insects. Vegetables such as artichoke or broccoli are almost impossible to de-infest completely. It is advisable to simply cut off and discard the top leafy parts, then clean and inspect the remaining sections before eating them or using them for cooking.

Problem nuts, flour, beans, and grains should be sifted, or soaked in water (the insects and other foreign matter float to the top).

SALAD-IN-A-BAG

Some salad purveyors promote vegetables that are pre-washed or are grown hydroponically, supposedly eliminating the insect problem. Regardless of these claims, always wash and inspect vegetables for insects.

PAREVE FOODS WITH MEAT OR DAIRY

While you can cook and eat pareve foods with any meaty or dairy dish, the pareve food always assumes the meaty or dairy status of the food it is cooked with or pot it was cooked in.

For example, if you add vegetables to a chicken soup, the vegetables become meaty and can no longer be eaten with dairy foods, and if you eat these vegetables you become meaty and must wait the designated time between eating meat and dairy (see "Day 19"). The same is true for the pareve foods that are cooked with dairy.

If a completely pareve food was cooked in a clean and empty meaty (or dairy) pot, it may be eaten without a waiting period between meaty and dairy (or dairy and meaty). However, since it was cooked in a meaty (or dairy) pot, the food cannot be eaten *together with* a dairy (or meaty) food (i.e., in a sandwich). It can, however, be served as a separate course during the same meal, being careful to use dishware that is of the same kosher status as the pot the food was cooked in (i.e., meaty or dairy).

If you bake a completely pareve cake using a clean and empty meaty (or dairy) baking pan, you do not become meaty (or dairy) by eating the cake. However, you should refrain from putting anything meaty (or dairy) directly on the cake (i.e., dairy ice cream).

Sharp pareve foods, such as onions, hot peppers, garlic, etc., that were cut with a meaty knife may not be eaten with dairy, and *vice versa*. This is because the biting sharpness transfers flavor in a way similar to how heat transfers taste.

FRUITS & VEGETABLES FROM ISRAEL

The Torah contains several commandments involving agricultural practices in the Land of Israel, include tithing the crops, resting the land during the seventh year, and not harvesting the fruit of young trees before the fourth year. These laws are known in Hebrew as *t'rumah*, *ma'aser*, *shmittah*, and *orlah*. Therefore, before purchasing fresh fruits and vegetables from Israel, make sure they have reliable kosher certification. The certification should indicate that the farmer and producer complied with all Biblical agricultural laws.

KOSHER EGGS

All raw and unfertilized eggs from kosher birds and fowl are kosher and considered pareve (neither meaty nor dairy). Kosher eggs are easily identifiable, since they are primarily round on one end and pointed on the other. Most commercially sold eggs today can be considered kosher and do not require kosher certification.

Since consuming blood is Biblically forbidden, you need to check the yolks of eggs before using them for cooking, frying, or baking to make sure they do not contain "blood spots." If you forgot to check them and accidently used the unchecked eggs for cooking or baking, set the food and utensils aside until you can ask an Orthodox Rabbi or kosher expert what to do.

The inspection of eggs for blood is performed by cracking each egg one at a time into a clear cup and inspecting the top, sides, and underneath for a red spot or blotch in the yolk area. If you find one, discard the egg, then thoroughly wash the cup used for inspection with cold water (hot water may cause kosher problems as heat transfers flavor). Note that naturally produced "organic" eggs produced on farms with roosters and hens are far more likely to have blood spots than mass-produced eggs.

You can boil several eggs at a time in a pot without inspecting them first for blood, relying on the fact that the majority of eggs are free of blood spots. If, however, you find blood in a cooked egg (i.e., a dark green or brown spot), you should discard the egg and put the pot it was cooked in aside until you can contact a kosher expert to find out what to do.

When boiling eggs, some have the custom to boil at least three eggs at a time. This is because if one egg had blood inside (and is thus not kosher) it would not render the other eggs (and pot) non-kosher, as it is nullified by the majority (the two other eggs). This also explains why some dedicate a specific pot for boiling eggs.

BLESSING BEFORE & AFTER EATING

For the proper blessing for fruits, vegetables, nuts, or eggs, see "Day 15."

TODAY'S ACTION
Replace the bread and baked goods in your home with kosher varieties.

DAY 23

Bread
& Baked Goods

*T*he aroma of baking bread is always enticing, especially before Shabbat and Jewish holidays when we bake delicious *Challah* (traditional braided bread). Many forms of nourishment and delectable enjoyment come from the modest mixture of flour and water. Breads, rolls, bagels, cakes, cookies, danishes, pastries — the list is as long and full as a meal itself. The Torah acknowledges bread's central place in our diets by calling it the "staff of life." The *Mishna* adds that *"without bread* *there is no Torah, and without Torah there is no bread"* (Avot 3:17). Unlike fruits and vegetables that are mostly ready for consumption as soon as they ripen, producing baked goods requires greater effort and exertion. In a symbolic way, we "partner" with God more noticeably here than with many other foods, by turning grains into edible and nourishing products.

BAKED GOODS & KOSHER

All grains in their natural state are inherently kosher and *pareve* (neutral, neither meaty nor dairy). Once grain is combined with other ingredients (i.e., flavorings, oils, emulsifiers, etc.), be sure that all ingredients, as well as all utensils and equipment, are kosher. Just as with any other food, baked goods loses its kosher status when non-kosher ingredients are used or if it is baked in a non-kosher oven. This is why you should only purchase baked goods that bear a kosher symbol from a recognized and reliable kosher certifying agency.

Before purchasing baked goods from a kosher bakery, make sure that the bakery displays an unexpired kosher certificate stating that it is under active and reliable kosher supervision.

PAS YISRAEL, PAS AKUM/PAS PALTER,

For bread to be permitted, a Jew has to bake it, or at least have some involvement that is integral to the baking process (i.e., kindling or adding to the fire in the oven). This not only applies to bread but also rolls, pretzels, cookies, and cakes — basically any food made with the flour of the five grains (wheat, barley, rye, oats, or spelt) and baked in an oven.

Pas (or *Pat*), in Hebrew, means "bread," and here it refers to all baked goods. The terms *Pas Yisrael*, *Pas Akum*, and *Pas Palter* refer to the level of kosher supervision and Jewish involvement in the baking process.

- PAS YISRAEL — Refers to all baked goods that were baked entirely by a Jew, or that a Jew had some involvement that is integral to the baking process (i.e., kindling or adding to the fire in the oven).

- PAS AKUM — Refers to baked goods that are baked entirely by non-Jews in a private, non-commercial setting. These are not permitted for consumption.

- PAS PALTER — Refers to commercially baked goods that are made with only kosher ingredients and baked on kosher equipment, but in non-Jewish industrial bakeries. Some *Halachic* (Jewish legal) authorities permit Pas Palter bread in situations where it is impossible (not merely "inconvenient") to find Pas Yisrael baked products.

All Rabbinic authorities agree that the kosher consumer's first choice should be Pas Yisrael over Pas Palter, and that those stringent in this area will be blessed. In places where Pas Yisrael is readily available (even if additional effort is required), Pas Palter is not permitted according to *all* authorities. By the way, most packaged baked goods on supermarket shelves bearing a kosher symbol are considered Pas Palter, unless the package specifically states "PAS YISRAEL" (or in Hebrew, פת ישראל).

THE MITZVAH OF "SEPARATING CHALLAH"

When baking using a certain quantity of flour and water, it is a *mitzvah* (commandment) to recite a special blessing, separate a small portion of dough (approximately 1 oz.), and set it aside to be burnt and discarded.

This mitzvah dates back to the Holy Temple in Jerusalem. The Jewish people would bring a gift from their first and their best food to the *Kohanim* (the priestly tribe). This gift was called *challah*. In remembrance of this gift, and in anticipation of the imminent arrival of Moshiach and the restoration of the Holy Temple services, we observe a version of this mitzvah today.

Our Sages tell us that the mitzvah of separating challah brings great blessings into the home. This is why Jewish women make an added effort to bake loaves of bread in honor of the Shabbat and Jewish Holidays (hence these loaves became known as "challah"). Since the challah may only be eaten by a kohein in the Holy Temple, the small portion of dough set aside today as challah is burnt to the point that it becomes inedible and then discarded.

HOW TO SEPARATE CHALLAH

- Challah is separated from dough made from flour of the following five grains: wheat, rye, barely, oat and spelt.

- Some have the custom to put a few coins into a charity box before separating challah, joining one mitzvah with another.

- For recipes that use less than 2 lbs., 11 oz. (about 7 cups) of flour, one does not have to separate challah.

- For recipes using between 2 lbs., 11 oz. and 3 lbs. 11 oz. (about 7 to 11 cups) of flour, separate challah *without* reciting the blessing below.

- For recipes using more than 3 lbs., 11 oz. (about 12 cups and up) of flour, and the liquid used is mainly water (not eggs, oil, juices, etc.), recite the blessing below and then separate challah:

בָּרוּךְ אַתָּה יְיָ, אֱלֹהֵינוּ מֶלֶךְ הָעוֹלָם, אֲשֶׁר קִדְּשָׁנוּ בְּמִצְוֹתָיו,
וְצִוָּנוּ לְהַפְרִישׁ חַלָּה:

Böruch atöh adonöy elohaynu melech hö-olöm, asher kid'shönu b'mitzvosöv,
v'tzivönu l'haf-rish Challah.

Blessed are You, Lord our God, King of the universe, Who has sanctified us with His commandments, and commanded us to separate challah.

Separate a small portion of dough (approximately 1 oz., or roughly the size of a small egg), and set it aside (some first hold the piece in their hand and declare "This is challah" before setting it aside). Wrap the separated piece of dough in foil and place it on a burner with the fire on, until it is blackened. If burning is not practical, you can dispose of it in the trash wrapped in foil or plastic.

BAKED GOODS WITH MEAT & DAIRY

Generally speaking, if all utensils, equipment, and ingredients used in the baking process are kosher pareve, you can eat the baked goods with either meaty or dairy foods. It is forbidden, however, to bake breads or rolls that contain meaty or dairy ingredients, since it becomes difficult to distinguish them rolls from pareve baked goods and they may accidentally be used with either dairy or meaty foods.

It is permitted, however, to bake cakes, cookies, pastries, and the like with dairy ingredients (i.e., cheese cake), but the goods must be identified as such. These dairy baked goods may not, of course, be eaten with meaty foods or served at a meaty meal, and if you are meaty (i.e., you just ate a meaty food), you must wait the required waiting period before eating the dairy baked goods (see "Day 19").

If you did not use any dairy (or meaty) ingredients, but only baked the cake or pastry in a clean meaty (or dairy) pan or oven, the cake can be considered pareve and may be eaten along with a meaty or dairy meal. However, care should be taken that it should not be served (or eaten) directly with meaty or dairy foods (i.e., for meaty, it should not be covered with dairy icing or ice cream, and for dairy, not dipped in meaty gravy or soup).

BLESSING BEFORE & AFTER EATING BREAD

Before eating bread or any bread product, one must wash their hands ritually with a large cup of water. The water is poured over each hand once (many have the custom to pour three times), and the special blessing "Al Netilat Yadayim," followed by the blessing of Hamotzi, is recited. The after-blessing is "Bircat Ha-mazon" (see "Day 15").

Baked goods that are not bread (i.e., cookies, cakes, pretzels, etc.) require the blessing of "Mezonot." The after-blessing is "Al Ha-michya" (see "Day 15").

DAY 24

Wine, Beer
& Whiskey

L'chaim! To life! In Judaism, wine is associated with holiness and sanctification. In fact, wine is often used for Jewish ceremonial purposes such as for *kiddush* (sanctifying Shabbat and Jewish holidays), for *kiddushin* (matrimonial ceremonies), and for many other holy occasions. However, since wine was also used by gentiles for idolatrous purposes, our Sages instituted protective measures to ensure kosher wine's spiritual purity, requiring that only Torah-observant Jews press the grapes and process the wine, all the way to the opening and serving of the finished bottle of wine. These measures also apply to grape juice and products containing grape derivatives.

SOME KOSHER WINE TERMS TO KNOW

There are three terms that describe the kosher status of wine or grape juice:

1) YAYIN NESECH (poured wine) — Refers to wine that has been poured to an idol or with idol worship in mind. This category of wine or grape juice is Biblically forbidden for Jews to drink or derive any benefit from.

2) STAM YAYNOM ("generic" gentile wine) — Refers to wine or grape juice that may not have been used for idol worship, but could have been touched by someone who believes in idolatry. This is enough to disqualify the wine, making it spiritually impure and forbidden.

3) MEVUSHAL (boiled wine) — Refers to wine or grape juice that was boiled prior to bottling. This action remedies the above problems, for in the Holy Temple cooked wine was disqualified from being brought on the altar and so it is not considered "sacramental wine." Therefore, according to most *Halachic* (Jewish legal) authorities, as long as the production equipment and any added preservatives or additives are kosher, the wine or grape juice is permitted even if touched by a gentile after it was boiled.

Luckily today, many domestic and imported kosher wines are already mevushal. When buying wine or grape juice, always check the label for a recognized and reliable kosher symbol and also for the word "mevushal" (or in Hebrew, מבושל).

Some pious Jews do not use mevushal wine for sacramental purposes (i.e., Kiddush) for the same reason that it was not permitted to be brought on the altar. Instead, they use non-mevushal wine that was produced exclusively by Torah-observant Jews and keep the bottle concealed until it is used. Even after opening the bottle it is kept concealed in a paper bag and poured only by observant Jews.

GRAPE INGREDIENTS IN FOOD

According to Jewish law, all liquids extracted from grapes, including grape juice, wine vinegar, and alcoholic beverages containing wine bases (i.e., cognac, brandy, vermouth), are considered as wine and must comply with the above requirements. Also, food products made with grape derivatives or flavorings (i.e., sodas, fruit punch, certain candy, and "Grapples") must bear a recognized and reliable kosher symbol.

BEERS

All unflavored beers, domestic and imported, that have no additives listed on the ingredient label are usually acceptable without kosher certification (as of this printing). "Lite" beers (i.e., low-caloric) often contain enzymes (which may be derived from non-kosher sources) and thus require reliable kosher certification.

WHISKEYS

Hundreds (if not thousands) of varieties of alcoholic beverages are available today. Some are inherently kosher because of their simple manufacturing process, containing only grain and other naturally kosher ingredients. Others are not kosher due to the use of non-kosher ingredients, equipment, or by being cured in non-kosher wine or sherry casks. The kosher consumer is therefore advised to only buy whiskeys that have a reliable kosher symbol on their label.

That said, many Halachic authorities recognize that most varieties of "straight" or "single malt" (not blended) whiskeys, including those from Scotland and Ireland, are inherently kosher, and thus permit their use even if they do not have a kosher symbol on the label. However, all other alcoholic beverages, such as liqueurs, brandies, cordials, and all flavored spirits must always bear a recognized and reliable kosher symbol.

Note: If the label on the bottle says that the product was aged in wine or sherry casks, sherry finish, dual cask finish, port finish, it should be considered non-kosher, unless it bears a reliable kosher symbol on the label.

AT THE BAR

Remember that condiments added to drinks at the bar, including olives, cherries, pretzels, chips, nuts, etc., must have reliable kosher certification. Furthermore, slices of lemon, lime, or other tart or acerbic fruit must only be cut with a kosher knife.

LIST OF COMMON KOSHER ALCOHOLIC BEVERAGES

For your convenience, below is a list of alcoholic beverages that are accepted as kosher (as of this printing). Remember to drink responsibly!

NOTE: We obviously cannot guarantee that the beverages on this list are still kosher at the time you will be purchasing them. It is advisable to always check with a kosher expert to be sure.

Gin

- All gin that do not contain any flavor additives.

Liqueurs

- Amaretto Disaronno
- Kahlua Liquor (only with OU)
- Bartenura
- Leroux line (most)

Rum

- Bacardi (unflavored varieties)
- Don Q Rum (only with OU)

Scotch (blended and single malt).

- B. Scotch/Single Malts
- Dewar White Horse Extra Fine
- Glenlivet
- Chivas Regal/Johnny Walker
- Glenfiddich
- J&B White Horse Fine Old

Straight Bourbon

- Bookers Maker's Mark
- Jim Beam
- Regular-white/silver.
- Jack Daniel's Wild Turkey
  Tequila

Vodka (grain or potato)

- All domestic (USA only) non-flavored vodka is acceptable.
- Belvedere Pravda (OU)
- Absolut Kettle One
- Chopin Stolichnaya

- Finlandia Vox
- Iceberg

- Grey Goose

Whiskey (including Canadian, Irish, Ryes)
- Bushmill's Irish (except Green label)
- Irish Jameson

- Crown Royal
- Seagram's (VO and 7-Canadian Blend only, not American blend)

BLESSING BEFORE & AFTER DRINKING WINE, BEER & WHISKEY

The blessing recited before drinking wine or grape juice is *"Hagafen."* The after-blessing is *"Al Hagefen"* (see *"Day 15"*).

The blessing recited before drinking beer or whiskeys is *"Shehakol."* The after-blessing is *"Boray Nefashot"* (see *"Day 15"*).

TODAY'S ACTION
Check your
medicine cabinet
and learn about
kosher miscellany.

DAY 25

Vitamins, Medications
& Miscellany

*B*y now it should be obvious that even vitamins and supplements require kosher certification. This is because they often include non-kosher animal derivatives such as gelatin, fats, and other non-kosher ingredients. For example, vitamins A and D are frequently derived from shark oil, and vitamin B is often made from animal liver, whey, and substances from a pig's stomach. Fortunately, many pharmaceutical

203

companies offer a wide variety of nutritional products and supplements with reliable kosher certification.

Regarding medicines, Jewish law draws a distinction between medicine that is taken to relieve symptoms or to cure an illness, and supplements that are taken proactively to maintain health and longevity. As the Torah values life so deeply, it mandates the suspension of its own prohibitions in order to save or restore life. With this in mind, the Torah permits the taking of medication that is derived from non-kosher sources in a situation where it is found to be medically necessary and there are no kosher alternatives. Consult a competent Orthodox Rabbi or kosher expert for guidance in such cases.

It is good to refrain from using flavored vitamins unless they have a reliable kosher symbol on the package.

KOSHER MISCELLANY

- Detergents and cleansers that are used for cleaning kosher dishes, cookware, and utensils (especially while using hot water) should only be bought if they have kosher certification, since many of these products contain lard or other non-kosher ingredients.

- Non-food items that are used in or around the mouth (i.e., mouthwash, tooth-paste, Chapstick, etc.) should preferably have kosher certification.

- It is a good habit to look for a kosher symbol on products otherwise thought to be "kosher benign" (i.e., plain bottled water [may have been processed on equipment used for other non-kosher drinks], etc.).

DAY 26

Kosher for
Passover

For a holiday that lasts just over a week around April each year, processed kosher foods inherit an added status: "Kosher for Passover." Even though products marked Kosher for Passover appear on store shelves as early as February or March, it is all in preparation for this short, eight-day holiday. The story of *Pesach* (Passover) is well known: how the Jewish people were slaves to Pharaoh in Egypt; how Moses led them out of bondage; how the Jewish people journeyed to Mount

Sinai where they received the Torah; and how they eventually entered the Land of Israel. In celebration and commemoration of the exodus from Egypt, the Torah commanded the Jewish people to celebrate the holiday of Passover.

Passover occurs every year, beginning on the 14th day of the Hebrew month of Nissan, the anniversary of the first exodus from Egypt. On this holiday, the Jewish people are Biblically commanded to eat *matzah*, "unleavened bread," and are prohibited from eating or possessing *chametz*, "leavened foods."

Thus, "Kosher for Passover" means that *in addition* to being "kosher," the product is free of chametz or chametz derivatives, nor was it prepared on non-kosherized chametz equipment.

Make sure that all packaged and processed foods purchased for Passover bear the words "Kosher for Passover" next to the kosher symbol of a well-known kosher certifying agency.

FROM THE TORAH

Immediately following the story of the exodus, the Torah declares: *"This day shall be for you as a memorial, and you shall celebrate it as a festival for God. For all generations you shall celebrate it as an eternal statute. For seven days you shall eat matzos, but on the preceding day you shall eliminate all leaven from your houses. For whoever eats leaven from the first day on will have his soul cut off from Israel"* (Exodus 12:14-15).

The prohibition against possessing and/or eating chametz on Passover is one of the most stringent commandments in the Torah.

WHAT IS CHAMETZ?

Chametz is a general term for all food and drink made from the five grains of wheat, barley, rye, oats, spelt or their derivatives which is leavened and, therefore, forbidden on Passover. Food that contains even a trace of chametz is prohibited.

CLEANING OUT ALL CHAMETZ

In the days or weeks leading up to Passover, we clean our possessions of chametz. In addition to cleaning every place in the house that may contain chametz, we clean the car, office, desks and drawers, clothing pockets, pocketbooks, purses, attaché cases, and any other areas where chametz may be found. We also check medicine cabinets since many medicines, sprays, and cosmetics contain chametz. We even check pet food ingredients to make sure they don't contain grain. If while preparing for Passover we find products that contain chametz, they should be discarded or locked away and sold (the room "leased" to a non-Jew for the duration of the holiday and the chametz sold [see below]; your local Orthodox Rabbi often does this for the community).

Any utensils used throughout the year for chametz food should either be properly kosherized for Passover or also put away in closets or rooms that are not easily accessible (locked or taped shut) and sold for the holiday.

THE MITZVAH OF EATING MATZAH

When the Jewish people hurriedly left Egypt, the dough they were carrying did not have time to rise, so our ancestors ate simple, flat, unleavened matzah. With only this unleavened bread as their provisions, they went into the desert faithfully relying on the Almighty for sustenance. Each year during Passover, especially at the Seders on the first two nights, we remember this "bread of faith" by eating matzah made from simple flour and water. In this way, we fulfill the Biblical commandment of *"Matzot shall you eat...."*

"SHMURAH MATZAH"

You may have heard or seen the term *"shmura matzah."* Shmurah, in Hebrew, means "watched" or "guarded," and describes matzah that is made from wheat that has been carefully protected from any contact with water, starting at the moment of harvest and continuing until the time it is baked into matzah. Shmurah matzot should be used for the three matzot of the Seder plate on both nights of Passover.

Shmura matzot are round in shape, kneaded and formed by hand for the express purpose of fulfilling the mitzvah of eating matzah. The matzot are made in a very stringent process under strict Rabbinical supervision. No more than eighteen minutes pass (the maximum time limit for leavening) from the moment that the water is mixed with flour to the time the finished matzah is removed from the oven. Furthermore, after each batch of matzah is made, every single piece of equipment is scrubbed clean in preparation for the next batch. The entire process completely eliminates the possibility of the flour becoming chametz at any time — from the cutting of the wheat through the end of the baking process.

Many people eat only shmura matzah (as opposed to the more common square "machine matzah") during the entire Passover holiday as an extra precaution against finding or eating chametz.

SHOPPING FOR PASSOVER

As mentioned above, all leavened foods made from wheat, barley, rye, oats, or spelt are chametz, and are prohibited on Passover. Obvious examples are bread, cake, cereal, spaghetti, beer, and whiskey. However, many products are not overtly chametz (i.e., apple sauce) but may have chametz ingredients or were made on chametz equipment. As another example, matzah used all year round may not necessarily be kosher for Passover. Therefore, you should only use matzot baked especially for the holiday. When shopping, remember to only purchase items that say "KOSHER FOR PASSOVER" (or in Hebrew, כשר לפסח), or have the letter "P" next to the kosher symbol (i.e., OU-p or OK-p), indicating they are kosher for Passover.

Raw fish, poultry, and meat are naturally Kosher for Passover, provided they have not come into contact with chametz, nor were prepared using chametz utensils; so are dairy products as long as they meet the same conditions. All whole fresh fruits and vegetables are kosher for Passover, as long as they, too, have not come in contact with chametz. During Passover, many people have a custom of only using fruits and vegetables that they can peel, since it is difficult to know for sure how the fruit or vegetables was packed, or what they came in contact with along the way.

The prevailing (Ashkenazic) custom is that on Passover one does not eat rice, millet, corn, mustard, legumes (beans, etc.) or foods made from these ingredients, since they sometimes can be confused for the five forbidden grains.

PREPARING THE KITCHEN

To prepare your kitchen for Passover, all chametz is removed or locked away in cabinets and sold. All surfaces that will be used for food preparation during Passover are cleaned and kosherized (or covered). Some people put aluminum foil or special covers on their countertops and other kitchen surfaces (i.e., cabinet shelves, refrigerator shelves, etc.), in case any chametz remains in a surface crack or corner.

In addition to cleaning and covering kitchen services, you also have to kosherize the sinks, stove, oven, microwave, dishes, silverware, pots, pans and other utensils that will be used on Passover, in order to purge them of any chametz.

To save time (and lots of effort), many people have separate sets of meat and dairy dishes, silverware, pots, pans, and other utensils strictly for Passover use. Some people even have a dedicated "Passover Kitchen," which is closed the rest of the year and opened only for Passover. Other people tape their chametz stove or oven shut for the holiday and instead use a portable cook top that is used only on Passover. You may want to contact your local Orthodox Rabbi to determine what will work best for you.

SELLING (DISPOSSESSING) YOUR CHAMETZ

To avoid possessing chametz on Passover, all chametz that one does not discard must be sold to a non-Jew for the holiday. This applies to all chametz that will not be eaten or burned before Passover and all chametz utensils that will not be kosherized. These are stored away in closets or rooms before Passover. This storage area is locked or taped shut and leased to a non-Jew.

Since there are many legal intricacies in this sale, only a competent Rabbi should be entrusted with its execution. The Rabbi acts as an agent both to sell the chametz to the non-Jew before Passover starts, and also to buy it back the night Passover ends.

Chametz that remains in the possession of a Jew over Passover may not be used, eaten, bought, sold, or even given as a gift after Passover.

PREPARING THE SEDER PLATE

Three matzot are placed one on top of the other on a plate or decorated tray. This symbolizes three ritual categories of Jews — Kohein, Levi and Yisrael. It also commemorates the three measures of fine flour that our forefather Abraham told Sarah to bake into matzot when the three angels visited them.

We place the following items on the cloth or tray:

1. *"Z'roa"* — The roasted chicken neck.

   Preparation: remove most of the meat from the neck of a chicken and roast it on all sides. It is symbolic of the Paschal (Passover) sacrifice brought at the Holy Temple in Jerusalem on the afternoon before Passover. It is not eaten.

2. *"Beitzah"* — The hard boiled egg.

   It symbolizes the festival sacrifice brought at the Holy Temple, in addition to the Paschal lamb. It is eaten before the main festive meal is served.

3. *"Maror"* — The bitter herbs (Horseradish root).

   It is symbolic of the bitter suffering of the Jews in Egypt. Eaten at specific points during the recital of the Haggadah.

4. *"Charoset"* — Mixture of chopped apples, pears, nuts, and wine.

   The mixture resembles mortar. It symbolizes the mortar used by the Israelites to make bricks while enslaved in Egypt. Used as a dip for the marror at specific points during the recital of the Haggadah.

5. *"Karpas"* — Some raw onion or cooked potato (some use parsley or celery). Eaten near the beginning of the Seder, and meant to intrigue the child.

6. *"Chazeret"* — bitter herbs (romaine lettuce leaves). Eaten as maror at specific points during the recital of the Haggadah and in the sandwich (koreich) later in the Seder.

*How the Kaarah (seder plate) is organized
(the three matzot are underneath)*

A DEEPER MESSAGE OF PASSOVER

For the Jews, "Egypt" represents more than just a place on the map. Egypt is a state of mind. The Hebrew name for Egypt is *Mitzrayim*, which is related to the word maitzarim, meaning "boundaries" and "limitations." To "leave Egypt" means to overcome those natural limitations that impede the realization of our potential.

The innermost essence of the Jewish soul is a spark of Godliness — infinite and unbounded. But the soul is in exile, in "Egypt" — restricted within this finite, material world. One person's Egypt may be most apparent in his selfish and base desires; another person may be enslaved to his rational mind. Passover empowers us to transcend limitations and realize the spiritual potential in every aspect of our lives.

When God commanded Moses to bring the Jewish people out of Egypt, He proclaimed: *"...they shall serve God upon this mountain"* Exodus 3:12). Our liberation was not complete until we received the Torah on Mount Sinai. God's Torah and commandments are the keys to achieving true freedom; freedom not only from physical enslavement, but from all our limiting beliefs and behavior.

The Torah shows us how to avoid the pitfalls that life presents us, and teaches us how to make this world a place of peace, harmony, and happiness for all humankind.

WHAT DOES "MATZAH" HAVE TO DO WITH LIBERATION?

The difference between leavened bread and matzah is pretty obvious: bread rises, while the Passover matzot are flat and not permitted to rise at all. Our rabbis explain that the "puffed up" nature of chametz symbolizes arrogance and conceit. The flat, unleavened matzah represents humility.

Humility is the beginning of liberation and the foundation of all spiritual growth. Only a person who can acknowledge his own shortcomings and submit to a higher wisdom can free himself from his own limitations. On Passover, we are forbidden even the minutest amount of chametz, symbolizing that we should rid ourselves of arrogance and self-centeredness. By eating the Passover matzot, we internalize the quality of humility and self-transcendence that is the essence of faith.

WE MAY HAVE LEFT EGYPT — BUT HAS EGYPT LEFT US?

On the seventh day of Passover, we commemorate the miracle of the splitting of the Red Sea — the culmination of the exodus from Egypt. With the Egyptian charioteers in hot pursuit, the Jewish people plunged into the sea. God turned the sea into dry land, creating walls of water on both sides, which allowed the Jewish people to pass through. Once the Jews were safely on dry land, the water returned to its normal state, drowning the Egyptians.

Our Sages explain that the splitting of the sea symbolizes yet another phase in our spiritual journey toward true freedom. Just as the waters of the sea conceal all that is in them, so does our material world conceal the Godly life force that maintains its very existence. Transforming the sea into dry land can be understood to mean revealing the hidden truth that the world is not apart from God, but is one with Him.

Often, however, after "leaving Egypt" — after overcoming our limitations and ascending to a higher level — we experience a rude awakening. We may have left Egypt, but Egypt is still within us! We still view life in terms of the values of a material world. We must strive to become aware of God's presence and influence in our lives, until "the sea splits" and our liberation is complete.

According to the Prophet Michah, God has proclaimed, *"As in the days when you left Egypt, I will show you wonders"* (Michah 7:15). The exodus from Egypt is the prototype for the final Redemption, when *Moshiach* (the Redeemer) will come, and slavery and suffering will be banished from the face of the earth.

This explains the reason that the verse states, *"As in the days when you left Egypt."* The exodus took place in one day. Why does the verse use the plural, "days"?

The answer is that true liberation is an ongoing process. The first steps out of "Egypt" are only the beginning. *"In every generation,"* our Sages tell us, *"and on each and every day, one is obligated to see himself as if he had gone out from Egypt that very day"* (Talmud, Pesachim 116b).

Therefore, all the lessons of Passover are really applied daily. We must rid ourselves of arrogance and become humble; we must deepen our awareness of God, as though the Reed Sea has split; and we must strive to improve our conduct, as befits the nation that received the Torah on Mount Sinai. Every step we take toward Torah and mitzvot brings us closer to the Messianic age.

PASSOVER & THE FUTURE REDEMPTION

The eighth day of Passover is traditionally associated with our fervent hope for the coming of Moshiach, the Jewish Messiah. The *Haftarah* (special reading from the Prophets) for that day contains Isaiah's prophecies about the Messianic era: *"The wolf will dwell with the lamb, the leopard will lie with the kid...they shall do no evil, nor will they destroy...for the earth shall be filled with the knowledge of God, as the waters cover the sea."* (Isaiah 11:6)

Maimonides cites the belief in Moshiach as one of the Thirteen Principles of our faith. He explains in his codification of Jewish Law (Mishneh Torah) that Moshiach is a Torah Sage who will lead the multitudes of Jewish people to the faithful observance of the Torah way of life. Eventually, he will rebuild the Holy Temple in Jerusalem, gather in the exiles to Israel, and usher in an age in which there is no hunger, war, jealousy, or strife.

In today's chaotic world, one may find the concept of imminent Redemption difficult to accept. We can take heart, however, from the story of Passover. Back then, despite our abject subjugation at the hands of the world's most ruthless and powerful nation — a nation from which not even a single slave had ever escaped before — redemption came swiftly, "in the blink of an eye," and we were free.

In recent times, we have witnessed events that even secular leaders have termed miraculous: the fall of communism, the miraculous protection that Israel had during its various wars, the exodus and ingathering of Jews to Israel from places of former oppression, the massive outpouring of aid to the victims of disasters, and the list goes on.

Today, the major nations of the world are indeed turning from creating weapons of destruction to looking for ways to promote mutual development and cooperation. In essence, they are beating the proverbial "swords into plowshares." Such developments strengthen our faith in Moshiach's imminent approach.

The last day of Passover is a uniquely appropriate occasion for our heartfelt prayers for Moshiach: *"Even though he may tarry, still I anticipate his arrival every day"* (Maimonides, Principles of the Faith, No. 12).

As Maimonides explains, it will be a time of peace and plenty for all humankind, a time when we will no longer have to struggle for a livelihood. *"In that Era there will be neither famine nor war, neither envy nor competition, for good things will flow in abundance and all the delicacies will be as plentiful as the dust. We will all be free to engage in spiritual pursuits to deepen our knowledge of God and serve Him unhindered."* (Maimonides, Laws of Kings, 12:5)

DAY 27

Restaurants, Travelling
& Kosher Out of the House

*T*he popular slogan "Judaism begins at home" follows with the lesser known "and is lived and observed on the road." The Jewish religion is not compartmentalized. The Jew is expected to observe his traditions everywhere. As mentioned earlier, unlike religions that reject and shun the physical world, Judaism turns every activity, including the most mundane, into an opportunity to connect with God (see "Day 2"). Therefore, if someone says, "I keep kosher at home, but when I am on the road I am not as careful," he or she has missed the point. Keeping kosher is about maintaining one's Jewish identity and the purity of one's Godly soul, elevating the world around them. Therefore, it makes no difference where one is — kosher is always observed.

EATING OUT

Eating in any food establishment, be it a meat or dairy restaurant, takeout grill, pizza shop, and the like, should generate a healthy dose of anxiety and concern for the kosher consumer. Honest kosher compliance is not easy to maintain in a busy commercial kitchen, and must be carefully planned and monitored by kosher experts.

At home in our own kitchens, we have total control of the food and ingredients we purchase and how they're cooked and prepared. But when eating out, this trust shifts to the owners and chefs of the food establishment. Therefore, we must make sure we are being sold what we are expecting: a strictly kosher meal.

As mentioned earlier, a "kosher" sign hanging in the window does not make an establishment kosher. This claim needs to be supported by a certificate from a recognized kosher certification agency that provides rigorous expert kosher training and sometimes even on-site supervision (required in many food establishments).

Some questions to consider:
- Are the owners and chefs as careful with kosher as I am at home?
- Who oversees the deliveries of raw foods and ingredients to ensure they are kosher and not mistakenly substituted for non-kosher varieties?

- Is there a qualified kosher expert on site ("*mashgiach*") supervising the cooking and preparation to ensure it is remains kosher?

- In a tight spot, does this establishment rely on leniencies that I would never consider for myself or my family?

- For meat establishments, are the meats and poultry "Glatt kosher"?

- In a dairy establishment, is the milk or cheese "Chalav Yisrael"?

- Are the breads, rolls, crackers, desserts, etc. "Pas Yisrael"?

Choosing only kosher places to eat out helped me rethink the places and entertainment I was frequenting in the first place!

CHARLES A., AGE 38
ATLANTA, GA

These are just a few of the questions that every kosher consumer needs to consider before choosing where to eat out.

Many kosher restaurants do have constant, reliable, and expert kosher supervision, and will display a current kosher certificate from a recognized kosher certification agency. Others are not so careful and may not have any supervision at all. The kosher consumer is therefore advised to inquire on the above by phone in advance, or in person, before patronizing the food establishment. Responsible owners or managers should be happy to provide answers in a respectful and knowledgeable manner.

EATING IN PRIVATE HOMES & AT PARTIES

One should use care and attention when eating away from home, including at private parties, business lunches, or even when having dinner at a friend's house (for people can be at different stages of kosher observance). Unless you know the degree of kosher followed in the purchase and preparation of the food, it pays to err on the side of caution (using tact and good sense, of course). This does not mean one should never eat out (although there are some who actually don't), only that one should be alert to the many kosher concerns and issues and to consult one's local kosher expert when in doubt.

CATERERS & PARTY PLANNERS

Whether you are invited to an affair, or are making one yourself, you should ensure that the caterer has satisfactory kosher certification and is adhering to kosher dietary law at the highest level. When catering in non-kosher facilities, for example, the process of kosherizing equipment, ovens, stoves, and warmers is very complex and can only be done by knowledgeable kosher experts.

Additionally, all served packaged and prepared foods must come from a kosher supplier that has its own valid kosher certification. Without expert kosher supervision, there are many ways things could fall through the cracks.

Party planners, especially those unfamiliar with kosher law, though well-meaning and -intentioned, may introduce non-kosher foods or items in take-home bags for guests, or, more subtly, use a favorite non-kosher additive or utensil, not realizing its critical impact.

TRAVELING & VACATIONS

Traveling while keeping kosher is easier nowadays than previously. Most local supermarkets offer thousands of food products with a kosher symbol from a recognized kosher certification agency, and many more sell unprocessed fruits and vegetables.

In addition, many companies now sell frozen kosher meals that can be double-wrapped and heated in any oven or microwave (see the "Travelling Kosher Q&A" below for how this is done). Some companies even offer self-heating meals, all you have to do is follow the directions and let the special packaging do the rest.

Airlines and many hospitals will often provide a pre-packaged kosher meal at no extra cost if requested in advance. Remember that any foods heated in a non-kosher oven should be served with its factory double-wrapped packaging intact; otherwise, it can no longer be considered kosher.

Many cities also have kosher restaurants and delis that are under reliable kosher certification. Often, the only foods that are difficult to find are fresh kosher baked goods and fresh meat or dairy products.

No matter where you are going or for how long, the secret of the well-seasoned kosher traveler is to plan your meals and shop accordingly before you leave.

Our best trips were those that I prepared for our kosher food needs well in advance.

ANNA, W., AGE 54
ST. LOUIS, MO

THE KOSHER TRAVELER'S PACKING LIST

- A variety of vacuum-packed kosher salami or cold cuts, and cheeses
- A box or two of matzah
- Favorite cookies or candy
- Self-heating meals
- Cans of kosher tuna, sardines, or other fish
- Frozen rolls or loaves of bread
- Microwaveable meals
- Nuts, raisins, peanut butter, jelly

KOSHER FOODS THAT YOU CAN COMMONLY FIND IN MOST SUPERMARKETS, MINI-MARKETS & AT REST AREAS

- Raw fruits and vegetables
- Juices and sodas
- Canned vegetables

- Chips, crackers, etc.
- Cereals and breakfast bars
- Frozen foods (i.e., knishes, pancakes, etc.)

Remember to look for a kosher symbol on any purchased processed food.

EXCLUSIVELY "KOSHER" VACATIONS

Many popular vacation spots have kosher establishments nearby to serve their growing Jewish tourist population. Today, one can even find first-rate kosher cruises. It pays to ask around and do a little online searching before you plan your getaway.

Additionally, some popular hotels are completely converted to kosher for Jewish holidays such as Sukkot, Chanukah, and Passover. In all cases, make sure their kosher certification is from a reputable and well-known kosher certifying agency.

SOME POPULAR "TRAVELLING KOSHER" QUESTIONS

Q: CAN I GET COFFEE OR OTHER HOT DRINKS ON AN AIRPLANE, OR AT A GAS STATION?

A: Yes. However, use your own cup (or a paper cup) and avoid offered milk or non-dairy creamers (they may be non-kosher). You should also avoid flavored coffees (unless they have a kosher symbol on the package), automatic coffee, cappuccino, and espresso machines since non-kosher milk comes out of the same pipes.

Q: CAN I BUY HOT PRETZELS OR POPCORN SOLD AT CONCESSION STANDS?

A: Only if the product and heating equipment are certified kosher. Look for a current kosher certificate from a well-known and reliable kosher certification agency. It is not enough to see a kosher symbol on the food package or store sign alone, since the heating equipment may have also been used with non-kosher food.

Q: CAN I GO INTO A NON-KOSHER RESTAURANT FOR A BUSINESS MEETING IF I WILL MAKE SURE NOT TO EAT ANYTHING OR EAT JUST FRUIT, OR EVEN EAT SOMETHING KOSHER I BROUGHT ALONG?

A: It is best to avoid this situation and find an alternative. In a case of real pressing need (i.e., one's livelihood is dependent on this meeting), one should seek the advice of a competent Orthodox Rabbi on what to do.

Q: WHEN AWAY FROM HOME, CAN I WARM FOODS IN A NON-KOSHER OVEN?

A: Yes. You must first make sure that the oven is completely empty and clean from any food residue or rust. You also have to double-wrap the food you are going to heat. This is done by tightly wrapping the food (or plate) with two layers of foil. When using a microwave, substitute paper or plastic for foil and make a tiny hole in a different spot on each layer to allow the steam to escape.

Q: CAN I GO TO ANY CAFETERIA, GET IN LINE, AND PURCHASE THINGS THAT I KNOW ARE KOSHER?

A: It is best to avoid this situation because of *Maarat Ayin* (creating an appearance of wrong-doing), as other Jews seeing you taking food would think all the rest of the food is kosher. When handling a packaged product such as a soda or bottled orange juice, or a box of kosher cereal, it is okay, as it is similar to going to the store to buy something. One, however, should not handle any serving trays, since it might appear to other Jews that a kosher food service is being offered, when in fact one is not.

Q: CAN I GO KOSHER AND STILL BE A VEGAN, VEGETARIAN, OR MACROBIOTIC?

A: Yes, you can be kosher on these diets. Just make sure to eat at least a little piece of chicken on Shabbat and Jewish holidays to fulfill the mitzvah of eating meat on those special days.

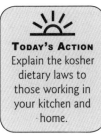

TODAY'S ACTION
Explain the kosher dietary laws to those working in your kitchen and home.

DAY 28

Domestic Help in the Kitchen

$\mathcal{E}$veryone appreciates help around the house, especially in the kitchen. Having another "pair of hands" when cooking, baking, serving, and of course cleaning up, can make all the difference. In a kosher kitchen you are responsible to make sure that the help understands basic kosher dietary laws, such as keeping meat and dairy (including their utensils) separate, and is prepared to consistently follow the rules. Otherwise, the help may well turn out to be a liability once you find that you

I let my help deal with all other chores around the house and keep the kitchen to myself.

LEAH P., AGE 44
LOS ANGELES, CA

have to re-kosher your kitchen because of a kosher "mistake" that you discovered (if you are lucky enough to discover it at all).

Therefore, before you let anyone work in your kitchen (either Jew or non-Jew), make sure to set clear ground rules. Even then, you are responsible for making sure that there are no lapses.

Even after being well educated about the kosher dietary laws, non-Jewish help may never be left alone in a kosher kitchen unless you are stepping out for a very short while, and they know you can come back at any moment, or they are aware that someone has the key and will check in from time to time.

The best idea is to keep things as clear and as simple as possible for your staff, leaving out the correct dishes, cutlery, sponges, towels, etc., so that they do not have to search for them, and possibly using the wrong item (i.e., meaty for dairy or dairy for meaty), jeopardizing the kosher status of your kitchen.

SPECIAL CONCERNS

- Making sure that non-Jewish help does not light a fire to cook or bake food from start to finish in your kosher kitchen (a Jew must light the fire and/or stir the pot). Otherwise the food (and pot) is considered non-kosher.

- Making sure the help does not mix meat and dairy utensils, sponges, dish towels, etc., especially when cleaning and washing up after a meal.

- Checking vegetables for insects, and eggs for blood spots may be done only by a kosher-observant Jewish adult.

- Making sure that non-Jewish help does not touch, open, nor serve "non-mevushal" wine (see "Day 24").
- Making sure the help does not warm up food that they brought from home in your kosher oven or use your kosher utensils.

DAY 29

Shabbat & Jewish Holidays

*J*udaism sanctifies time as well as space. For example, by celebrating Shabbat (the Sabbath) every week, we testify that God created the world. Similarly, we find many days throughout the year connected with Jewish observances that enrich our lives both spiritually and physically. These auspicious days begin at the start of the Jewish year with Rosh Hashanah, Yom Kippur, and Sukkot, and continue with Chanukah, Purim, Passover, and Shavuot. Every holiday, including the fast days such as *Tisha B'Av* (9th of Av), emphasizes the historic and continuing bond between God and the Jewish people.

Living Jewishly includes living with an awareness and anticipation of upcoming Jewish holidays and observances. More than just an opportunity to enjoy good food and good company, these sanctified days help us connect to our Jewish heritage and nourish our Godly soul much as keeping kosher does, ultimately even elevating the mundane weekdays that come in between.

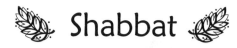

Shabbat

A SANCTIFIED ISLAND IN TIME

From the dawn of creation, the seventh day of the week, Shabbat (Hebrew for "rest") was set aside as a spiritual island in time. For the 25 hours of Shabbat, the Jewish people cease interacting with mundane activities. We stop working and creating, moving and shaking, to create a space where we can acknowledge the true Creator, remembering that all fortunes come from God, and realizing that our work is just a vessel to receive His blessings. Shabbat is where it all happens.

Shabbat is more than the day on which God rested from creating the world. It is a day when we connect to our spiritual Source, a day on which we stand proudly as Jews, proud to be God's light unto the nations.

The *Talmud* declares that *"Shabbat is equivalent to all the mitzvot"* (*Yerushalmi Berachot* 1:15, *Shemot Rabah* 25:16). By keeping Shabbat, we attest to the truth of all the fundamental principles of our faith: creation of the world by God, Divine Providence, Divine Prophecy, etc.

Yet, a richly satisfying Shabbat never just happens. It is the result of effort made all week long.

FOOD & SHABBAT

The Torah calls Shabbat "delight" for very good reason. No Shabbat is truly complete without delicious *challah* (traditional braided bread), tasty wines, exquisite courses of fish, poultry or meat, and enchanting desserts. A Shabbat meal is one that is truly fit for a king.

According to our Sages, it is a positive *mitzvah* (commandment) to put out the best food on Shabbat. The Talmud relates that Hillel, one of our foremost Sages, would shop all week with an eye to honor Shabbat. Whenever he saw a special food in the market, he would buy it and say, "This is for the Shabbat." When he found something of better quality, he would replace the earlier item and say, "This is for the Shabbat." Thus, his whole week was permeated with Shabbat!

My children learned to cook and bake by helping me prepare for Shabbat.

CHANA G., AGE 43
MIAMI, FL

THE SHABBAT MEALS

There are three meals served on Shabbat: Friday night dinner (full dinner); Shabbat lunch (full lunch); Shabbat late afternoon (light dinner).

Since it is Biblically forbidden to cook, bake, or heat food on Shabbat, all food items must be prepared before the onset of Shabbat (Friday, before sunset). To learn how to keep foods warm in a permissible manner, consult your local Orthodox Rabbi.

Common traditional Shabbat foods are:

- Kosher wines
- Gefilte Fish (ground fish patties)
- Chicken Soup (Friday night)
- Dessert of fruit, candy, or cake

- Challah (braided bread)
- Salads
- Chicken or Brisket.
- "Cholent" (beef stew) and cold-cuts or cutlets (Shabbat day).

Of course, all the food, wine, and beverages served, including all dishes and serving utensils are kosher. This also means making sure that only meaty utensils are used at meaty meals, and that all desserts are *pareve* (neither meaty nor dairy).

KEEPING AN AUTHENTIC SHABBAT

Keeping Shabbat authentically is one of the most transformative experiences in a Jew's life. Shabbat is such a singularly extraordinary day that even those who have already been observing Shabbat for many years can discover something new and beautiful to learn, practice, and share with friends and family.

There are numerous books on the many aspects of Shabbat. Most of them are available at your nearest Jewish bookstore or online. For a start, see the Laws of Shabbat section of the "Code of Jewish Law." Don't pass up any opportunity to learn more about this great heritage!

QUICK OVERVIEW OF SHABBAT OBSERVANCES

The commandment to observe Shabbat is repeated in the Torah many times and with great emphasis. One of the better known passages about the Shabbat is included in the Shabbat morning prayers: *"And the children of Israel shall keep the Shabbat, as an everlasting covenant. It is a sign between Me and the children of Israel forever: That in six days God made heaven and earth, and on the seventh day He ceased from work and rested"* (Exodus 31:16-17).

About Shabbat, the Sage Maimonides writes as follows: *"The Shabbat is the everlasting sign between God and the people of Israel. He who observes the Shabbat properly, honoring it and delighting in it to the best of his ability, is given a reward in this world, over and above the reward that is reserved for him in the World to Come"* (Maimonides, Laws of Shabbat 30:16).

More than anything else, it has been the Shabbat that has distinguished the Jewish people from all other nations of the world, for Shabbat observance is not just a matter of a single precept or custom, but something that is fundamental to the Jewish religion and Jewish way of life.

During Shabbat, a Jew not only refrains from work, closes down his store, factory, or workshop, and halts all work at home, but is completely transformed into a person of holiness, devoting time to prayer and study, and quality time with his family. Even externally this transformation is in evidence, in one's dress, eating, walking, and talking.

Jews make the Shabbat and Shabbat makes the Jewish people. That is what is meant by referring to the Shabbat and the Jewish people as soul mates. Indeed, more than the Jewish people have kept Shabbat, the Shabbat has kept the Jewish people, for more than anything else, the Shabbat unites all Jews in all parts of the world.

SHABBAT IS MORE THAN A "DAY OF REST"

Shabbat is not merely a day of rest, a day of "quiet time" to rejuvenate our energies. While this may also be the case, rest on Shabbat means the cessation of any creative function normally done during the week. By ceasing such "creative work," we relinquish our control over our environment, thereby making space where we can recognize and appreciate God, the Creator of everything.

Practically (and very generally), this means that on Shabbat, Jewish people are prohibited from performing any activity associated with the Torah's list of 39 general categories of creative *melacha* (activity). These include lighting fires (i.e., cooking, baking, heating, driving a car, turning lights on or off, using electronics such as phones, fax machines, computers, watching TV, etc.), sewing, handling money (i.e., shopping, doing business), plus activities that are not in the "spirit of Shabbat," such as going to the movies, playing golf or tennis, rowing, swimming, skating, boating, flying, etc.

What's left to do?

A young person came to a Rabbi and asked, "Why are there so many restrictions on the Shabbat? I feel so imprisoned! I can't watch TV, I can't use the phone, I can't turn on lights, I can't go to the mall."

"Did you hear me emphasize the negative?" the Rabbi asked.

"What do you mean, Rabbi? You taught us that you can't do this and can't do that, and that is how one guards the sanctity of the Shabbat."

The Rabbi replied, "My son, what I said was that on Shabbat you are permitted *not* to watch TV, *not* to answer the phones, *not* to check for e-mail, *not* to cook, etc. I taught you about experiencing genuine rest as outlined in the laws of Shabbat of the Torah. Try it and you'll see it is most liberating, not imprisoning!"

Indeed, when was the last time that you felt free to shut out the world and be yourself with your friends, family, and, yes, your Creator? That's what Shabbat is all about!

After observing Shabbat and "tuning out" the world and "tuning in" to your family and spirituality, you'll feel the happiness, satisfaction, and fulfillment that Shabbat offers everyone who observes it properly.

My husband and I now look forward to Shabbat every week. You have to experience it to really appreciate it.

JULIE B., AGE 34
TEMPE, AZ

PREPARING FOR SHABBAT

Our Sages relate that Shabbat "takes" from the Friday before and extends into the Saturday night after. We don't just spring directly into Shabbat; we have to prepare ourselves beforehand. At the same time, we don't end Shabbat on the dot of sunset on Saturday, but bring some of the Shabbat atmosphere with us into the Saturday evening.

CLOTHING

It is customary to have special clothes for Shabbat. Traditionally, this means a white shirt and suit for men and boys, and a modest dress for woman and girls. In fact, many people set aside their nicest suit or dress and wear it only on the Shabbat. In that way, it's obvious to all that Shabbat is a special day.

FOOD

As mentioned above, we enjoy three meals on Shabbat. The table is traditionally draped with a white tablecloth. Some place the Shabbat candles (before Shabbat) on the dining table (or elsewhere in the room) in order to enjoy the radiant light of the Shabbat candles during the meal. The finest cutlery, dishes and silverware are also brought out and used. The meal is enjoyed as much spiritually as it is physically, with the sharing of words of Torah as well as the joyous singing of Jewish songs.

SPIRITUAL GROWTH

We spend a part of Shabbat in prayer, a part studying Torah, and a part enjoying the people who are important to us. Shabbat is also an opportune time to do "spiritual accounting." We focus on how we can better ourselves during the week to come.

FAMILY

Shabbat has been called "the glue that keeps the family together." On this day, families spend time eating and sharing thoughts with one another. It is also customary for parents to learn topics of Jewish values with their children during Shabbat.

SHABBAT CANDLE LIGHTING

It is a custom for Jewish women over Bat Mitzvah (age 12 and up) to light candles every Friday evening, eighteen minutes before sunset (see your local Jewish calendar for the exact time). Many women light two candles, one representing the Biblical commandment to "Remember the Shabbat" and the other representing the commandment to "Guard and Observe the Shabbat." Some women add a candle for each child. This beautiful tradition of kindling a candle for each child expresses the thought that every person is unique and brings a special light to the world.

In many homes, girls over the age of three (and even earlier) light their own candles. In that case, the child lights first so that the mother can help her do it safely and properly.

To light Shabbat candles, ignite the wick(s) of the candles at the appropriate time (but *never* after sunset on Friday), then draw your hands three times around them, drawing the light toward your face. Cover your eyes with your hands, and recite the appropriate blessing (found in most prayer books).

"HAVDALLAH"

After Shabbat ends (when at least three stars are visible in the sky), we say the *havdallah* ("separation") blessings over a cup of wine or grape juice, along with a special blessing over fragrant spices and a multi-wicked flame of a candle. The havdallah blessings mark the separation of the holy day of Shabbat and the days of the coming week. (See your local Jewish calendar for the exact time to recite havdallah.)

Jewish Holidays

The celebration and observance of Jewish holidays are determined by the Hebrew calendar, which follows the lunar cycle. The Jewish year begins with the month of Tishrei (in early fall), and is counted consecutively from the first year of creation nearly 5,800 years ago.

Below you will find a brief and basic overview of Jewish holidays as they occur during the year. Each holiday has its own rituals and obligations which are too detailed to fully cover here. Consider the information below as an introduction, and make a point to study more fully about each holiday before it arrives.

Rosh Hashana (Tishrei 1-2)

The two-day holiday of Rosh Hashanah marks the Jewish New Year and is celebrated with tremendous awe and solemnity. On Rosh Hashanah, we coronate

God as our King. On this day, God examines the deeds of every Jew and those of all mankind. Our Sages tell us that based on this evaluation, God determines the personal and global fortunes of the future year.

On the eve of Rosh Hashanah we light candles. Special prayers are offered in the synagogue over both days of Rosh Hashanah, including the sounding of the shofar ("ram's horn") which each Jew is obligated to hear.

Customs Relating to Food:

- We serve round challah (traditional braided bread), often containing raisins, to celebrate the circular cycle of leaving one year and entering a new one. The raisins express our wishes that the new year be a "sweet" one.

- We dip challah into honey at the beginning of the meal.

- We dip an apple in honey and eat it at the evening meal on the first night of Rosh Hashana, and recite a special prayer.

- We serve sweet foods such as carrot *tzimmes*.

- On the second night of Rosh Hashana, we eat a new (meaning, not eaten this season) fruit, say the proper blessing over it, and recite the blessing of *Shehechiyanu*, thanking God for allowing us to reach this season.

- Some people place the head of a fish or lamb on the table as a symbol of blessings at the head of the year (may we be a "head" and not a "tail").

Yom Kippur (Tishrei 10)

Yom Kippur, the "Day of Atonement," is the holiest day of the Jewish year. On this day, we fast and spend as much time as possible in prayer. The purpose of the day is to express our regret over past misdeeds and our resolve to do better in the future.

It is on this day that God pardoned the Jewish people from the sin of the Golden Calf. Ever since then, it has remained the day of supplication on High. If our repentance is done with sincerity, followed by concrete positive action, God recognizes our regret and completely forgives and wipes away our sins.

From a few minutes before sunset on the day leading into Yom Kippur, until after sundown the next day, Jews are Biblically commanded to refrain from eating or drinking any food or drink, washing their bodies, using perfumes and ointments, wearing leather shoes, and engaging in marital relations. Candles are lit on the eve of Yom Kippur before sunset, and all work-related restrictions relating to the Shabbat apply to Yom Kippur as well. Special prayers are recited all day in the synagogue.

Customs Relating to Food:

- On the day leading into Yom Kippur (*Erev* Yom Kippur), it is a mitzvah to eat two festive meals to provide strength to fast. The first meal is eaten early in the afternoon, and the second just before the onset of the fast.

- We dip challah into honey at the beginning of the meal.

- Fish is traditionally served in the first afternoon meal. Meat is not served in either meal because the salt in the meat can make one thirsty. Poultry, however, is permitted.

- It is customary to eat *Kreplach* (triangular dumplings filled with ground meat usually served in soup). These pockets symbolize the covering of "severity" with "loving kindness."

- Fish and dairy food are not served in the second meal. Salads, soup, and poultry may be served.

- Spicy or overly salty foods are not recommended.

Sukkot (Tishrei 14-21)

Following the solemn days of Rosh Hashanah and Yom Kippur, we celebrate Sukkot, the "Festival of Booths." Sukkot is also known as the "Season of Rejoicing."

Sukkot is one of the *Shalosh Regalim*, the "three pilgrimage festivals" when historically all Jews would travel to the Holy Temple in Jerusalem to pray and serve God. Sukkot, lasts for seven days, and work is not permitted on the first two days.

The word *sukkah* is Hebrew for "booth," and refers to the Biblical commandment for Jews to dwell in man-made huts for the duration of the holiday. A sukkah is an outdoor structure whose roof is made of *s'chach* (Hebrew for "vegetation"), such as palm fronds, evergreen, or bamboo. The sukkah symbolizes the "clouds of glory" that surrounded and protected the Jewish people during their forty years in the wilderness.

Another mitzvah associated with the holiday is taking the "four species," i.e., the *lulav* (palm branch), *etrog* (citron), *hadas* (myrtle), and *aravah* (willow).

Customs Relating to Food:

- We serve traditional festive meals on the first two days of the holiday.

- It is a mitzvah to eat all meals in the Sukkah.

- We say a special blessing over eating in the Sukkah.

- We dip challah into honey at the beginning of the meal.

Hoshana Rabbah (Tishrei 21)

Hoshana Rabbah is the last day on which we fulfill the mitzvot of the four species and make a blessing on dwelling in the sukkah. The day is referred to as Hoshana Rabbah (literally, the great *Hoshana*) because of the additional *"Hoshana"* prayers that are recited in the synagogue. It is also considered to be the final day of the New Year's Divine "judgment" in which the coming year's fate is determined. It is therefore customary to recite the entire book of Pslams and stay up all night on the eve leading into Hoshanah Rabbah to study Torah.

Customs Relating to Food:

- It is customary to eat a festive meal in the afternoon.

- We dip challah into honey at the beginning of the meal.

- It is customary to eat *Kreplach* (triangular dumplings filled with ground meat, usually served in soup). These pockets symbolize the covering of "severity" with "loving kindness."

Shemini Atzeret & Simchat Torah (Tishrei 22-23)

Shemini Atzeret is "the eighth day of assembly." It is a time when the Jewish people and God celebrate their unique relationship.

Every Shabbat during the year, during the morning services in the synagogue we publicly read one portion of the Torah from a Torah scroll. On Simchat Torah (Rejoicing with the Torah), we read the final portion and begin reading the Torah from the beginning once again. To celebrate this event, all the Torah scrolls are brought out from the ark, and the men and children sing and dance with them with great joy.

Those living in the land of Israel celebrate Simchat Torah on Shemini Atzeret. In the Diaspora, Simchat Torah occurs on the day after Shemini Atzeret.

Customs Relating to Food:

- We serve traditional festive meals (i.e., fish, meat or chicken, and wine).

- On Shemini Atzeret, it is a custom to eat all meals in the sukkah. (However, we do not make the special blessing on eating in the sukkah.)

- We resume dipping challah into salt at the beginning of the meal.

- Before sunset, a "farewell" snack is eaten in the sukkah, as the mitzvah of dwelling in the sukkah draws to a close as night descends.

- On Simchat Torah, we do not eat in the sukkah.

Chanukah (Kislev 25 - Tevet 3)

Chanukah, the Festival of Lights, recalls the miracle that took place over two thousand years ago (165 BCE), when a handful of Jews called the Maccabees defeated the enemies of the Jewish people. At that time, the Greeks considered themselves to be the "enlightened of all the nations" and forbade the practice of supra-rational *mitzvot* (commandments) by Jews. They mocked our ancestors' faith in mitzvot that did not have a "logical" basis, being observed solely because God so commanded (i.e., the kosher dietary laws, circumcision, Shabbat, etc.). The Greeks succeeded in secularizing many Jews, luring them to exchange their "old" faith for the "new and enlightened" ways.

Due to the Maccabees' heroic and uncompromising dedication to their faith, God put success in their hands. The small band of Maccabees defeated the mighty Greek army and successfully returned to Jerusalem to restore the service in the Holy Temple.

When the Maccabees arrived and attempted to rekindle the great Menorah, they found only enough undefiled olive oil to burn for one day. Miraculously, the lights in the Menorah burned for eight days, signaling God's Divine pleasure and renewed protection.

To celebrate the great miracle of Chanukah, Jews around the world kindle a menorah in their homes each year beginning on the 25th of the Hebrew month of Kislev, starting with one light, and adding another on each night of Chanukah, until the entire menorah is illuminated.

What ultimately became of the all-powerful Greeks, including the "modernist" Hellenized Jews? They disappeared to history. We must never forget that it was the dedication of the Maccabees who steadfastly held to their faith and did not compromise their traditions and religion to "fit in" that kept Judaism alive, surviving to this day. It is our commitment and dedication to keeping Judaism real and relevant in our lives that will ensure the same for all our future generations.

Customs Relating to Food:
- It is customary to serve foods cooked or fried in oil (i.e., donuts, potato pancakes, etc.) to recall the miracle of the oil.

- It is also customary to eat dairy foods to commemorate the heroic act of Judith of Betuila. She killed the Greek general who besieged her town by getting him drunk after plying him with salty cheese.

Purim (Adar 14)

Purim is another Jewish holiday that celebrates the victory of "right over might" and "light over darkness." In the days of Mordechai and Esther (356 BCE), the wicked Haman, an advisor to King Ahasuerus, attempted to annihilate the Jewish people.

As told in the *Megillat Esther* (the scroll of Esther), the Jews turned to God in prayer and rededicated themselves to Torah and mitzvot. As a result, God delivered them from their enemy. The story of Purim is a fascinating story of palace intrigue, ambition, hate and greed, and finally the triumph of goodness and righteousness over evil. But much more than that, it shows that God is always watching over His people, and even when all hope seems lost, one must remember that God provides personal Divine supervision.

Purim is celebrated with festivity and joy. The reading of the Megillah is required to be heard twice, once at night and once during Purim day.

On the day of Purim, it is a mitzvah to give people presents consisting of at least two ready-to-eat foods. These are called *"Mishloach Manot."* We also eat a festive meal on Purim afternoon and give charity to at least two poor people.

Customs Relating to Food:

- We eat *"hamantachen"* pastry, filled with apricot, raspberry, or poppy seed.

- We send food presents called *"Mishloach Manot"* to family and friends.

- A festive meal is served on Purim afternoon.

Passover (Nissan 15-22)

Pesach, or Passover, commemorates the exodus of the Jewish people from Egypt more than three thousand years ago. It is also known as the "Season of Our Freedom." Passover is also one of the *Shalosh Regalim*, the three pilgrimage festivals, when all Jews traveled to the Holy Temple in Jerusalem to pray and serve God, lasts for seven days, and work is not permitted on the first two and last two days.

On the first and second nights of Passover, during the traditional Passover Seders, we read the Haggadah, which recounts the redemption from Egypt and included praises for God for saving His people. We also eat special foods associated with the seder.

Customs Relating to Food:
Chametz (leavened) food is not eaten all of Passover. Only food that is kosher for Passover may be eaten (see "Day 26").

Foods needed for the Seder (in addition to your dinner menu):

- Matzot (ideally Shmurah Matzot) — 3 matzot per person.
- Kosher wine (for the four cups) — 4 cups per person.
- Onions, potatoes, or parsley (for karpas) — 1 per 6 people (approx.).
- Chicken neck (for z'roa) — 1 for each Seder plate on the table.
- Cooked eggs (for the beitza) — 1 for each Seder plate on the table and enough for each person to have one to start the meal.
- Maror I (for the maror) — Romaine lettuce (2-4 leaves p.p.).
- Maror II (for the maror) — Ground horseradish root (1.20 ounces p.p.).
- Charoset (for the maror) — Mixture of ground apples, pears, nuts, and wine. Small amount for each Seder plate. (Usually homemade).

Shavout (Sivan 6-7)

This holiday is also one of the *Shalosh Regalim,* the three pilgrimage festivals, when all Jews traveled to the Holy Temple in Jerusalem to pray and serve God.

In the days of the Holy Temple, the Jewish people brought the first fruits of their harvest as offerings. It also marks the day that the Torah was given to the Jewish people at Mount Sinai.

On the Festival of Shavout, we hear the reading of the Ten Commandments in the synagogue, and eat a festive meal at home.

Customs Relating to Food:

- It is customary to eat dairy foods on the first day of Shavout.

Days of Fasting

There are seven communal fast days on the Jewish calendar. Four out of the seven recall the destruction of the Holy Temple in Jerusalem, which marked the beginning of our current exile.

Fasting, according to our Sages, helps stir our hearts so that we can focus on improving our performance of Torah and mitzvot and on becoming closer to God. Since food and drink are physical needs, by refraining from them it is easier to focus on more spiritual matters. Additionally, by abstaining from food we notice our mortality and more greatly appreciate our dependence on God.

All Jews, including Jewish boys over 13 and girls over 12, fast. Pregnant or nursing women, including someone who requires medication, should consult an Orthodox Rabbi for guidance as to how to properly observe these fast days.

Fast of Gedalia/Tzom Gedaliah (Tishrei 3)

This fast recalls the assassination of Gedalia ben Achikam (423 BCE), a noble Jewish governor who attempted to rebuild and maintain Jewish settlements in the Holy Land after the Holy Temple was destroyed by the King of Babylon. His untimely death was seen as a sign that the exile would continue into the foreseen future.

The fast begins at daybreak and ends after nightfall.

Yom Kippur (Tishrei 10)

Yom Kippur is the Day of Atonement (see "Yom Kippur" earlier in this chapter). The fast begins before sunset and continues until after nightfall of the following day.

10th of Tevet/Asara B'Tevet (Tevet 10)

On this day, Nebuchadnezzar, the King of Babylon, laid siege to Jerusalem, beginning the chain of calamities that ended in the burning of the Holy Temple. The fast begins before daybreak and ends after nightfall.

Fast of Esther/Taanit Esther (Adar 13)

This fast commemorates the fast that Queen Esther undertook during which she prayed to God to repeal Haman's decree to annihilate the Jewish people (see the holiday of "Purim" above).

On this day, towards evening, we give *"Machatzit Ha-shekel"* in the synagogue. This is a half-dollar coin which is given to charity. It recalls the half-shekel coin given by the Jews during the month of Adar. It was used to purchase communal sacrifices in the Holy Temple.

The fast begins before daybreak and ends after hearing the reading of *Megillat Esther*, the "Scroll of Esther," after nightfall.

Fast of the Firstborn/Taanit Bechorim (Nissan 14)

This fast commemorates God sparing the Jews when He struck the Egyptian first-born during the tenth Plague in Egypt. It is observed by firstborn males over the age of 13. A father is responsible for fasting for his firstborn son until his son reaches that age.

The fast begins before daybreak and ends at the Seder. However, those who are fasting traditionally attend a completion of a tractate of *Talmud* during the day, as the festive occasion nullifies the fast.

17th of Tammuz/Shiva Asar B'Tammuz (Tammuz 17)

On this day, Moses broke the first set of Tablets because the Jews made and worshipped the Golden calf. Many years later, the walls of Jerusalem were breached by enemy armies on the same day, ultimately leading to the destruction of the Holy Temple on the 9th of Av. This day begins the period known as the "Three Weeks."

During the three weeks between the 17th of Tammuz and the 9th of Av, we do not cut our hair, and we refrain from listening to music or getting married as a sign of mourning over the destruction of both Holy Temples. During the last nine days of the three week period (the 1st to 9th of Av), the mourning observances intensify and we refrain from eating meat, drinking wine, wearing freshly laundered clothes (except on Shabbat), and taking baths or showers for pleasure.

The fast begins before daybreak and ends after nightfall.

9th of Av/Tisha B'Av (Av 9)

This is the saddest day on the Jewish calendar. It marks the day of the destruction of the First and Second Holy Temples. In addition to the above, many other calamities befell the Jewish people on this day.

On *Tisha B'Av*, the Jewish people refrain from eating or drinking, washing their bodies, using perfumes and ointments, wearing leather shoes, and engaging in marital relations. From the onset of the fast until the middle of the next day, we sit on low stools to further show our mourning. We also read the book of *Eicha* (Lamentations) in the synagogue.

The fast begins before sunset the previous day, and lasts until after nightfall of the following day.

Our Sages state that God Himself fulfills the laws that He gives to the Jewish people. According to one of these laws, it is forbidden to destroy a synagogue. The only exception is for a site that will be used to rebuild a bigger, more beautiful structure. Similarly, the destruction of the Holy Temples will soon be seen as a prelude to the building of the Third and everlasting Holy Temple.

May we merit to see the rebuilding of the Holy Temple and the ingathering of the Jewish people to the Holy Land through our righteous Moshiach, speedily in our days.

DAY 30

Going Kosher:
Ready, Set, Go!

*Y*ou've made it to the 30th day! Be proud of yourself for taking concrete steps to make Judaism relevant to your life. If you haven't already done so, now is the time to put any remaining steps of going kosher into practice. Over the course of reading this book, you've learned the power of the essence of food: how in a world of contrasts, just as a billionth of an atom of polonium can devastate a human body, the essence of kosher food can fortify the body and enliven the Jewish soul. You've

253

also learned that kosher observance is inexorably tied to your Jewish identity, and how keeping kosher allows you to express your pride in your religion every time you eat.

Know that your ancestors are smiling in Heaven, secure that their prayers for an unending line of Jewish descendants is being fulfilled through you.

CHECKLIST & SUMMARY OF THE THIRTY DAYS

- ☐ Study the Biblical sources of the kosher dietary laws.
- ☐ Become aware of the spiritual aspects of eating food.
- ☐ Get in touch with a relative or friend who observes kosher.
- ☐ Let go of any false notions you may have about the kosher dietary laws.
- ☐ Familiarize yourself with basic kosher concepts and ideas.
- ☐ Familiarize yourself with different kosher terms.
- ☐ Learn what's involved in "going kosher."
- ☐ Consider the interpersonal effects of "going kosher."
- ☐ Time to make a practical plan of action.
- ☐ Take some first steps in observing the kosher dietary laws.
- ☐ Plan the kosherizing of your kitchen.
- ☐ Learn what can be kosherized, must be bought new, or given away (part 1).
- ☐ Learn about and perform the immersion of your utensils in a mikvah.

- ☐ Begin reciting blessings before and after eating or drinking kosher food.
- ☐ Take the "Kosher Shopping Quiz" and learn about buying kosher food.
- ☐ Familiarize yourself with the different kosher symbols on food packaging.
- ☐ Visit your local kosher butcher, baker, and grocer.
- ☐ Replace the meats and poultry in your fridge with kosher varieties.
- ☐ Replace the milk and dairy products in your fridge with kosher varieties.
- ☐ Replace the fish and fish products in your fridge with kosher varieties.
- ☐ Learn about "neutral" foods that are neither meat nor dairy.
- ☐ Replace the bread and baked goods in your home with kosher varieties.
- ☐ Refresh your bar with only kosher wines, beers, and whiskey.
- ☐ Check your medicine cabinet and learn about kosher miscellany.
- ☐ Learn about special Passover food observances.
- ☐ Start eating in kosher food establishments.
- ☐ Explain the kosher dietary laws to those working in your kitchen and home.
- ☐ Learn about the special day of Shabbat and other Jewish Holidays.
- ☐ Time to tackle those things you've pushed off to "later" and go completely kosher.

PARTING TIPS

- Now is as good a time as ever to call your local kosher expert or Orthodox Rabbi to go over any remaining questions you may have, and to set a date to kosherize your kitchen (if you haven't done so yet).

- If you find you are still "sitting on the fence" with going kosher, try introducing some of the simple first steps listed in "Day 10."

- Keep this book handy and study it again.

- Pass this book along to a friend!

Inspirational Reading

 Easing Into Kosher

by Leah Lederman

A few years ago my family and I entered a new phase of our Jewishness: we began keeping kosher. This was not a quick or easy decision; in fact, it wasn't until it became clear to me that, as a Jewish woman, I could no longer live any other way, that we made the commitment. I had reached the point where I could not reconcile certain contradictions in our lifestyle. My husband and I had made a point of calling our daughter by her Hebrew name, we fasted on Yom Kippur, and we ate matzah on Passover. But in my eyes, this display of our Jewish identity seemed empty without the integration of Judaism into our daily lives, which keeping kosher provides.

257

Now, after two years of keeping kosher, I still cannot put into words how precious kosher living has become to me.

I derive a great sense of personal fulfillment and satisfaction from knowing that keeping kosher is part of my life. The sense of control I have gained from keeping kosher has spread into every area of my life. As a family, we have been drawn together more closely in indefinable ways — in ways which I can only attribute to the role keeping kosher plays in our lives.

At this point, although my family and I cannot even imagine eating foods which were basic components of our diet three years ago, the transition still seems new. And in some ways, the transition is not yet over, for we are always learning and growing.

There is no denying that, in one way or another, keeping kosher maintains an important status in the soul of every Jew. And it is precisely the importance kosher plays in the life of a Jew which can make the transition to kosher seem intimidating.

In my case, the seeming myriad of intricate laws and differences in custom, the traditional stereotypes of kosher food as bland and limited, the social pressures of business, family and friends — all combined to create looming obstacles, despite the urgency of my need to keep kosher.

With my husband and young daughter, I encountered and overcame these fears. We read books, had family conferences, and encouraged each other until the obstacles that had separated us from kosher life fell away one by one. Together we entered a world in which we found as much variety in culinary experience and social opportunity as we had previously enjoyed — in some cases creating new opportunities not only for our cooking practices, but also our social encounters.

As a family, I think our greatest fear about keeping kosher was that of losing our culinary identity. I myself grew up in the southwest United States, which may have the most non-kosher cuisine in the world. We enjoy cooking and eating a wide variety of foods, and with each new cookbook or inspiration I acquired, we went through periods of eating Indian food, Chinese food, gourmet, macrobiotic, Mexican, etc. Yet keeping kosher, rather than limiting my cooking abilities, expanded them.

The first and most obvious challenge kosher presented was how to continue to cook our old favorites, but keep them kosher. Through experimentation, substitution, and the advice of friends, I discovered that there was very little, if any, sacrifice involved in using new versions of my favorite dishes. And thanks to the "vegetarian phase" I went through prior to my marriage, I had plenty of vegetarian recipes which needed little or no adaptations to meet kosher requirements.

In addition, there are a number of very good kosher cookbooks with recipes that extend kosher cooking to many types of cuisines. The constantly growing availability of foods with proper kosher supervision has encouraged me to cook a variety of foods which range from fish sticks to miso-lentil burgers to Beef Wellington.

I would like to close with the hope that kosher becomes as strengthening and positive an experience for you as it has been for our family. Just remember, you're not alone. There are thousands of families and individuals who have translated their lifestyles into the world of kosher. Each time you see someone searching for a kosher symbol in a supermarket, buying matzah for Passover, or asking for advice at a kosher meat store, your awareness of the link between you and all other Jews will become stronger and more precious. So relax, take your time, and enjoy.

(Reprinted with permission from "Body & Soul: A Handbook for Kosher Living")

Does God Really Care What I Eat?

by Tzivia Emmer

Keeping kosher is making a comeback. Across the United States and wherever Jews live, people are discovering or strengthening their commitment to the thirty-three century-old dietary laws of the Jewish people.

If we had asked the average Jew living about a hundred years ago if he or she kept kosher, a likely answer would have been, "Of course! I'm Jewish!" For our great-grandparents, keeping kosher was as natural as the act of eating itself. Very few people departed from the practice even when their observance in other respects may have slipped.

In the transition from Europe to America and after the upheavals of this century, the situation almost completely reversed. Many of us grew up thinking that Jews who still kept kosher were quaintly anachronistic, much like the Amish with their horses and buggies. We assumed that kosher was an obsolete health precaution, valid in the days before refrigeration, but no longer meaningful. Our great teacher and

260

prophet Moshe Rabbeinu (Moses) was presumably then a kind of early FDA administrator, and the prohibitions against eating milk and meat together, or consuming swine and shellfish, according to this newly-minted view of keeping kosher, had to do with bacteria, trichinosis, sanitation or the like.

If anyone had told us that kosher was a *mitzvah* (commandment) of the Torah, given to the Jewish people by God at Mount Sinai and designed to help form a nation whose mission it was, and still is, to bring Godliness into the world, we would have been quite incredulous, even indignant.

"What do you mean, bring Godliness into the world?" we might have replied. "Why should God care what I eat? The important thing is to be a good human being. What does food have to do with it?"

Such questions still form the backbone of modern objections to kosher, and make possible the notion that the dietary laws are hygienic in origin.

The questions may be valid, but they are not Jewish. In the European world of our forebears, the question of whether God cares what we eat did not come up — not because they were less intelligent or sophisticated than we are, and not because they didn't have refrigerators, but because their world was a totally Jewish one. It was permeated with Jewish values and Jewish ideas about the nature of man, God and the universe.

A change in milieu has brought about a total change in thinking. We are immersed in a culture that assumes a perspective which is sometimes diametrically opposed to that of Judaism. Non-Jewish thought has so pervaded Western civilization that we have come to think of its values as neutral, even universal. But they are not.

It is difficult therefore for the contemporary mind to grasp just why Judaism makes such a big deal over eating and drinking, basic necessities which are shared not only by all mankind, but by animals as well.

Prayer, meditation, charity, and an ascetic lifestyle are recognized by all as being "religious." According to the prevailing view, the soul is spiritual and holy while the body is material and contemptible. (The flip side of this is hedonism, where the body itself is worshipped.) In any case, why should God care what I eat?

The Torah tells us to *"know Him in all your ways."* The Hebrew language does not even have a word for "religion." The Jewish view is that not only on Shabbat or Holidays, and not only in prayer, but at all times we have the power to sanctify daily existence. The Jewish home is called a miniature sanctuary. The table is considered an altar.

Each of the commandments, many of which involve physical objects (kosher food, Shabbat candles, *tefillin, mezuzah*), serves as a channel or connection between a Jew and God. Each mitzvah performed strengthens this connection. Physical existence, exemplified by the body, is neither spurned nor glorified for its own sake, but elevated and refined in the service of the soul. The physical world itself is a vehicle for bringing holiness into the world.

Kosher provides an opportunity to be truly human, for only man can exercise choice and self-discipline in satisfying physical desires.

The food we eat is absorbed into our flesh and blood, directly affecting all aspects of our being. Birds of prey and carnivorous animals have the power to influence the eater with aggressive attributes, and they are among the foods forbidden by the Torah.

For a Jew, non-kosher food dulls the mind and heart, reducing the ability to absorb concepts of Torah and mitzvot, including even those mitzvot that can be understood by human intelligence. Forbidden foods are referred to in the Torah as abominations to the Godly soul, elements that detract from our spiritual sensitivity. One becomes less sensitive to feelings of Godliness, and less able to understand Godly concepts. Conversely, when one eats kosher food, one's receptivity to Godliness is enhanced.

The kitchen takes on a new dimension when we think of the awesome responsibility involved in providing kosher meals for one's family. The spiritual well-being of our spouse, children, guests, and by extension the entire Jewish people depends on upholding the kosher dietary laws. Although a thorough investigation and continued supervision are necessary when a commercial product is declared kosher, no *mashgiach* (expert religious kosher supervisor) peers into the pantry or watches the pots and pans used in a Jewish woman's kitchen.

Does God care what I eat? The connection of kosher to the essence of the Jewish soul, in each individual and in the entire nation, should provide an answer. God does indeed care what I eat.

(Reprinted with permission from "Body & Soul: A Handbook for Kosher Living")

 My Journey

Vivian Perez

"Why keep kosher?" was the foremost question on my mind ever since I decided to do something concrete about being Jewish. I used to pester my rabbi, Rabbi Yehoushua Binyomin Rosenfeld of Colombia, with that question at every possible opportunity, and he would always take the time to explain, yet again.

As newlyweds, my husband and I started to attend the rabbi's weekly Jewish studies classes. I remember looking questioningly at the rabbi, never being quite satisfied with any of the reasons given as to why I should observe kosher. None of the answers seemed to justify changing my accustomed eating habits. Until one day — I don't really remember how — but I made the decision to just jump in. I decided I was just going to do it even though I still didn't understand it completely.

I'm not an impulsive kind of a person – quite the opposite, in fact. But something deep inside made me just dive in and begin keeping kosher. In that moment (I didn't truly realize it then) I felt that I dove into the comforting waters of kosher living.

As anyone who has ever gone deep-sea diving knows, it is only after you're enveloped by the sea that you begin to see and appreciate its hidden beauty.

Only after I actually started feeling beholden to and observing the kosher dietary laws did the answers begin to come. Surprisingly enough, they didn't come from outside; they came from somewhere within. The more meticulously I kept kosher, the deeper the answers from within resounded.

At first, I remember how joyous I was to feel my "Jewish essence." Every time I ate, I was reminded of my identity – my Jewish soul. Something that was once so physical had become so spiritual. I was awed at discovering that we can master such self-control, commitment, and purpose. I was experiencing and feeling how observing kosher captivated my entire life. In fact, my perspective on life had changed. No longer was I questioning and analyzing everything, for I felt that everything in creation was analyzing me.

Life was never going to be as trivial, as routine, as "dry" as it was before I committed myself to going completely kosher. It marked the beginning of the entry into the sea of inner knowledge.

Through observing the kosher dietary laws in my day-to-day life, I came to understand what life is really about: there is a Creator. He knows our anatomy because He designed it. And He knows that the Jew has a holy soul which must be nurtured and guarded. There is physicality and spirituality. Each person has a holy soul and an animal soul. There are permissible foods and non-permissible foods. Just as we know that the air we exhale is only as good as the air we inhale, so too, what comes out of us through our thoughts, speech, or actions is influenced by what goes in.

Now that I observe the Jewish dietary laws, I think back on my eating habits before my observance with the following analogy: Think of the finest automobile in the world, and one day deciding to fill up the gas tank with heavy, leaded gasoline. After all, no one should dictate to me what to put into "my" car. It's mine. I can do what I want! And after the "fill up"? Maybe the car is still all shiny outside, but the engine just doesn't perform to its potential. For me, that's how I understand kosher.

Observing kosher has liberated my soul. No longer a spectator, it became the protagonist in my life. My soul sought to express itself not just at appointed food intervals, but in every conduit of the body, filling the body with divine purpose. Even in mundane, day-to-day dealings, I realized that there are "kosher" and non-kosher ways to conduct affairs, and I became sensitive to going about my life in a kosher manner.

To me, kosher observance is like "The Declaration of Independence" for the soul. To express, expand and permeate the depths of the kingdom, which is the body.

To think of the kosher dietary laws as just a grueling regiment with routine requirements and regulations, is like telling a professional diver in full scuba gear to stay close to the shore, to not dive beyond the shallow waters. That's how frustrated my soul felt when it was not given the fuel needed for its realization.

So, take the dive. Once you do, keep on going, deeper and deeper. Allow yourself to become enwrapped in the ocean and to see what magical beauty will reveal itself from within your own soul that you may never have known you had.

P.S. Thank you Rabbi Yehoshua, the Lubavitcher Rebbe's emissary in Colombia, for motivating my soul to take the first dive.

 A Set of Dishes

Dr. Velvl Greene

Even before we met Rabbi Moshe Feller in 1962 we would have been considered active and even committed Jews. Most of our friends were Jewish, our families were Jewish, our interests included Jewish "things," and our outlook was certainly Jewish.

We read books published by the JPS, we listened to Jewish records, we treasured the Chagall prints in our home, and were dues-paying members of a Conservative synagogue. Gail was a leading soprano in the synagogue choir and I was one of the very few members who attended on most Friday nights, regardless of whose bar mitzvah was being celebrated that weekend. We were probably Zionists, too. We regularly contributed to the UJA, attended our city's *Farband* picnics, and were officers on the board of Herzl Camp.

Before we met Rabbi Feller, however, I don't remember doing anything deliberately, or for that matter, abstaining from anything deliberately, because and only because it was a Torah commandment. Such thoughts never really entered my mind. One went to synagogue and lit candles and ate *gefilte* fish and wore a *tallit* (prayer shawl) because it was a traditional thing to do, and a pleasant tradition at that. Not to do so would be making a statement of denial, or of disinterest, or of apathy. I didn't care to deny or to be disinterested. It wasn't part of my self-image. On the other hand, we didn't keep kosher or refrain from driving on Shabbat, or any of those other things. They were simply not relevant. They played no role in my value system.

Note that we were not consciously protesting or transgressing, as one hears the early Jewish socialists or freethinkers having done. Those would be statements that we didn't care to make. We were, quite simply, "good American Jews" who didn't want to make waves. Of course, we knew that some Jews avoided non-kosher food and didn't drive on Shabbat. (There were remarkably few of them in our town, then.) And those were their traditions and their choices. We didn't think they were wrong — only slightly behind on the social evolution scale.

Looking back at those simpler days, I think that our lives reflected the characteristic paradox of the modern secular Jew: interested in Jewish things but basically ignorant; active in Jewish circles but limited in choice; committed to community, family, profession and the "Jewish People" but quite unaware of the foundation that informs this commitment. And above all, quite devoid of the learning and experience which permit discrimination between significance and triviality, reality and fraud. There must have been thousands like me. There still are. You see them arriving in Israel by the bus-load in "young leadership groups" or "fact finding missions" or "synagogue tours." They are too committed to the global picture to worry about the Jewish survival of their own children, or even themselves.

Actually, if we hadn't been in this kind of pattern ourselves, we probably wouldn't have met Rabbi Feller. He sought me out because I was a potentially rising star of the Jewish community. He was trying to organize his first banquet and wanted my name as well as others like me on his sponsors' committee.

The story of our first meeting has been told often enough (it was even mentioned in *Time* magazine) to obviate the need for retelling. On the surface it looked like a comedy. A strange, bearded, black-hatted young man remembers, just before sunset, that he has not yet said his afternoon prayers. Disregarding the fact that he is in my office, that he had asked for the appointment, that he is requesting a favor — he stands up, walks to the wall, ties a black cord around his waist and proceeds to mumble and shake. I will never forget my bewilderment and embarrassment. I didn't know what he was doing or why. I didn't know Jews prayed outside a synagogue. I didn't know they prayed in the afternoon. I didn't know they prayed on weekdays. And I didn't know how anyone could pray without someone announcing the page!

There were a lot of things I didn't know, then. But I did develop a definite interest and a special affection for this young man who was so pleasant and so different. He had a completely different set of rules to guide him — at once so radical and so archaic. He not only marched to the beat of a different drum — he seemed to enjoy the music more than we did ours. Above all, he was committed and consistent. I related to that. It is a beautiful trait in a world of laissez-faire religion and situation ethics.

In a short time we became friends — his family and ours. We discussed, we debated, we visited, we socialized. Gail and I were impressed with their sincerity and genuine warmth, but we still thought of them as anachronisms — as remnants of a past, as out of tune with the realities and needs of the modern American world. We didn't change our lifestyle because of them. Instead we kept waiting for them to change theirs. After all, nearly everyone else who had started out with a beard and hat ultimately did.

If he tried to influence us, during those early months, it must have been a very subtle effort. There was certainly no overt pressure or demand. Of course, they wouldn't eat at our house. But that wasn't a signal that something was wrong. They were so far out that their dietary idiosyncrasies were the least things one noticed. We started studying together, but our progress was infinitesimal. I asked too many questions, challenged too many axioms. I was definitely not a compliant student. It could have gone on like this for a long time, if it weren't for our trip to Warsaw.

In the summer of 1963 I was invited to participate as a member of the American delegation in an international conference on space research in Poland. My balloon-borne samplers had discovered viable microorganisms in the stratosphere at a time when the field of exobiology was too full of speculation and embarrassingly lacking in real biological data. Whatever the real reasons for the invitation, it was an opportunity to be grabbed. In 1963, visits to Warsaw and Eastern Europe were very rare. Few of my professional colleagues had been to Warsaw since the war; none of my Jewish friends, certainly.

Gail and I left the three children with my parents in Canada and we flew to Warsaw. It was a dismal visit. In those years the city had not yet recovered from the destruction of World War Two. Physical destruction was evident in the piles of rubble that covered huge sections of the city. The emotional destruction was worse. The indigenous Polish anti-Semitism which had been fueled generously by the German occupation was now being nurtured by the Jew-hatred of the new Russian masters. We were told that there were a few thousand lonely Jews left in Warsaw: a handful of Jewish Communists, some of whom we met in the office of the Yiddish newspaper; less than a handful of old men who attended services in the only synagogue left standing; several in the performing arts; and the rest who had returned from the camps after the war and didn't want to leave their dead and/or their memories. They had survived the war and now they were surviving the peace.

One evening we attended a performance in the Jewish Theater. It was an edited version of *Tevye the Milkman* in Yiddish. The only part of the script written by Sholem Aleichem that remained described the misery and pogroms of the Tzarist times. The rest of the play dealt with the promise of the coming Soviet revolution. The hero of the play was not even Tevyeh. As one can imagine, it was Tevyeh's son-in-law Feferl, the revolutionary who was exiled to Siberia. It made no difference. We were the only ones in the theater who listened to the performance. The rest of the audience was a tour group from Sweden who were listening to a simultaneous translation with earphones.

Even twenty years later, I still remember the chill (it was the middle of June) as we walked through the area where the ghetto had once stood. The walls and all the buildings had been leveled. Piles of stone and burned timbers still lay there. But one could see where the streetcar tracks had ended because a wall had once been built across them. And it was possible, with the aid of maps we had copied from Holocaust literature, to recognize the original street lines, and even their identities. We could find our way to the Umschlagge Platz, to Mila Street and to the old Jewish cemetery.

I remember crying at the tomb of I.L. Peretz, the great Jewish writer after whom the day school I attended in Winnipeg was named. I remember crying at the large mounds of earth that covered unmarked mass graves. I remember walking a lot and crying a lot. This, after all, was the Jewish heritage that I knew. There, but for the luck of somebody emigrating in time, was my home or my grave. This was the end of the Yiddishist, Socialist, Zionist, European Judaism knew. I was affected more by Warsaw than I would be ten years later by the Yad Vashem Holocaust Memorial in Jerusalem. The latter is a more beautiful monument, tastefully done. It is a museum, a history lesson, a shrine, an antiseptic display. Warsaw was death and cultural annihilation.

Through it all, I wondered how Gail was being affected. After all, I was a product of the "Old Country" culture of Winnipeg. She came from the sterile culture of Southern California's Reform temples. Peretz and Sholem Asch and Warsaw were part of my upbringing. How was all of this moving her?

I found out on Saturday afternoon. We had visitors — a Polish Jew and his two children whom we had met at the cemetery and whom we invited for tea. We had heard that there was a Jewish school and wanted to hear more about it. He, it developed, was looking for a handout. The seven-year-old child knew nothing. The eleven-year-old proudly recited the sum total of his Jewish knowledge: the four questions from the Passover *Haggadah*. We drank tea. I gave them a gift and my business card, and they left. Then we both cried. The end of Warsaw's centuries of Jewish creativity was a little boy who could barely stammer out "*Mah Nishtanah.*"

Then Gail reacted. She sat up on her bed where she had been crying and spoke the most firm words I had heard in our seven years of marriage:

"I don't know what you think and I don't really care, but I've made up my mind. As soon as we get back, I'm going to ask Moishe to make our house kosher. We're the only ones left. There's no one else. If we lose it, if we don't do it, if our children don't know about it, there won't be any Jews anymore. You can do what you want. But our house is going to be Jewish."

It was a defiant proclamation and she meant it. The pictures, the books and the music were not enough. She intended to transform the house organically, its very essence. Moreover, she was as good as her word. When we arrived in Minneapolis, the first person she called was Rabbi Feller, and he was only too willing to comply.

I don't remember all of the details. But I do remember the shocked look on his face when he first looked into our refrigerator. To this sweet young man, fresh out of the *yeshiva*, non-kosher meant a scar on the pleura of the animal who supplied the meat; or one drop of milk in fifty drops of chicken soup. The sight of real pork and shellfish must have been shattering. But bit by bit he "put our house in order." He introduced us to a kosher butcher; he taught us to look for the kosher emblem on packaged food; he spent hours boiling silverware and metal utensils; he supervised the blowtorching of our oven; Mrs. Feller helped Gail buy new dishes.

One item gave him trouble: an expensive set of English bone china which we had received as a wedding gift from my sisters in Canada. It was a beautiful set and without doubt, one of our more precious possessions. Gail was quite eager to "kasher" the dishes by soaking and heating. She wanted to use them for Shabbat. I'm sure the whole project would have ended if she had been told then that the only way to kasher china, even English bone china, is to break it. He didn't have the heart to destroy our china. Or maybe he was a better psychologist than we took him for. When he discovered these dishes and what foods they had been used for to serve, he suggested that we put them away. "Don't use them until I ask about such things in New York. Someone in New York must have more experience with things like this than I do."

They were put away. Every time he returned from a New York trip, Gail would ask what he had learned. And each time he had "forgotten." But he would be sure to remember next time. In the meantime, "Make sure they are put away in a safe place. You haven't used them, have you?"

This went on for months; then for years. The china was on display but it was never used. We kept waiting for expert advice that never came. Somehow, life went on without Minton Twilight in Grey.

We became closer to the Fellers during those years. Slowly the transformation which started in the kitchen moved into other areas of our life. Rabbi Feller introduced us to the Lubavitcher Rebbe, and we started growing in observance. Gail stopped singing in the synagogue choir; I started to put on tefillin sporadically at first, a little more regularly later on. I stopped driving on Shabbat. A few months later, so did Gail. We stopped eating at McDonalds. One Shabbat, we didn't switch on the television altogether. We bought a pair of tzitzit for the little boy. We switched membership to a synagogue with a *mechitzah* separating the men and women. Gail started going to immerse in the *mikvah* (pool of water set aside for ritual immersion). A few steps forward; a little backsliding; more steps forward. Years.

But the English bone china remained in the cabinet. Until one day, I came home from the university, and it was gone....

It was after a series of traumatic and melancholy miscarriages. Before observing *taharat ha'mishpacha* (the laws of family purity), it seems we had no difficulty having healthy and normal children. But when the mikvah became a feature of our family life, we started having trouble — three miscarriages in four years. Gail was sad; I was sad. Our friends comforted us. The Rebbe wrote letters of encouragement to Gail — private letters which I still have not read. But when I came home that singular day, she was smiling again:

"I took the china next door and sold it to Dorothy (our Gentile neighbor). Then I took the money and bought this *shaitel* (wig). What do you think of it?"

All this happened about 15 years ago. In 15 years you buy and discard a lot of *shaitlach*. Our two older daughters grew up and got married. They live with their husbands and their own children in Jerusalem. The little boy recently completed his

Rabbinic studies in the Lubavitch yeshiva in Montreal. We had two more children since then — the delights of our middle age. We have grown, both of us, both personally and professionally.

And we have another set of English bone china, from which we eat every Shabbat.

(Reprinted with permission from Chabad.org)

The Kosher Toolbox

Recommended Reading

A GUIDE TO THE KOSHER DIETARY LAWS, Rabbi M. Morgan
C.I.S., Lakewood, NY

BRACHOS STUDY GUIDE, Rabbi Eliezer Wenger
B'Ruach Hatorah Publications

BODY & SOUL: A HANDBOOK FOR KOSHER LIVING, Lubavitch Women's
Cookbook Publications, Brooklyn, NY

ILLUSTRATED GUIDE TO JEWISH LAW: The Kosher Kitchen
Feldheim Publishers, Brooklyn, NY

IS IT KOSHER?, Rabbi Eliezer Eidlitz
Feldheim Publishers, Brooklyn, NY

KASHRUS AND THE MODERN KITCHEN, Rabbi Halperin
Oratz Publishing

KASHRUT - BACKGROUND AND REFERENCE GUIDE, Rabbi Y. Lipschutz
Mesorah Publications, Brooklyn, NY

KEEPING KOSHER IN A NON-KOSHER WORLD, Rabbi Eliezer Wold
Shmuel Whol, Brooklyn, NY

MEAT AND DAIRY, Ehud Rosenberg
Mesorah Publications, Brooklyn, NY

TEVILATH KEILIM, Rabbi S. Eider
Targum Press, Southfield, MI

THE CODE OF JEWISH LAW, Rabbi Shlomo Ganzfried

THE JEW AND HIS HOME, Rabbi Eliyaho Kitov
Sheingold Publishers, New York, NY

THE KASHRUS MANUAL, Rabbi Shmuel Rubenstein
Israel Bookshop, Lakewood, NJ

THE KOSHER KITCHEN, Rabbi Rafael Abraham and Cohen Soae
Bene Aharon Publishers, Jerusalem

THE LAWS OF KASHRUS, Rabbi Benyomin Forst
Mesorah Publications, Brooklyn, NY

THE NEW PRACTICAL GUIDE TO KOSHER, Rabbi S. Wagschal
Feldheim Publishers, Brooklyn, NY

GREAT KOSHER COOKBOOKS
SPICE AND SPIRIT: THE COMPLETE KOSHER JEWISH COOKBOOK
Lubavitch Women's Cookbook Publications, Brooklyn, NY

SPICE AND SPIRIT KOSHER PASSOVER COOKBOOK
Lubavitch Women's Cookbook Publications, Brooklyn, NY

KOSHER BY DESIGN, Susie Fishbein
Shaar Press, Brooklyn, NY

KOSHER BY DESIGN: Entertains, Susie Fishbein
Shaar Press, Brooklyn, NY

KOSHER SHORT ON TIME, Susie Fishbein
Shaar Press, Brooklyn, NY

PERIODICALS
The Kosher Spirit, O.K. Kosher Labs
(877) 266-5641 - Brooklyn, NY
www.KosherSpirit.com

KASHRUS Magazine, Subscriptions
(718) 336-8544 - Brooklyn, NY
www.KashrusMagazine.com

לזכות
הרב הת' יוסף בן חי' מלכה
מרת חנה פריווא בת אלטער יהושע הכהן ע"ה
ומשפחתם

לזכות
הירשל פסח בן טשערנא
רייזא פייגא בת דבורה
ומשפחתם

לזכות
הרב הת' שניאור זלמן בן חנה פריווא
מרת דבורה גבריאלה בת רייזא פייגא
חנה פריווא בת דבורה גבריאלה
הינדא גאלדא בת דבורה גבריאלה
דוד משה יהודה בן דבורה גבריאלה
ומשפחתם

לזכות
מנחם מענדל בן מרים שרה
מניא שיינא בת מרים שרה

the
jewish
LEARNING GROUP

We provide easy direction and instruction for leading an enjoyable observant Jewish life. We publish exceptionally easy-to-understand and practical guides on Jewish law and custom, as well as traditional prayer texts with clear transliteration and instruction, as well as many other items geared specially for the beginner.

Over the past decade, our popular products have spread around the world helping thousands of Jewish people in more than 14 countries. From Ann Arbor, Michigan, to Oklahoma City, Oklahoma; from the official Passover Seder of the White House staff, to the halls of Oxford University.

We are very proud to have our innovative educational products so enthusiastically embraced by lay people, rabbis, and teachers around the globe.

We encourage you to give our guides to your family, friends, and to purchase them for your synagogue and school — deep bulk discounts are always available!

Visit our online web-store to browse and order from our exciting library
www.JewishLearningGroup.com
or call us at 1-888-565-3276

www.JewishLearningGroup.com
1-888-56-LEARN

BULK ORDERS WELCOME